Report on Experience

Report on Experience

John Mulgan

Edited by Peter Whiteford
Preface by Richard Mulgan
Foreword by M. R. D. Foot

Frontline Books, London

Victoria University Press

Naval Institute Press
ANNAPOLIS, MARYLAND

This edition published in 2010 by Frontline Books, an imprint of
Pen and Sword Books Ltd, 47 Church Street, Barnsley,
S. Yorkshire, S70 2AS.
Visit us at www.frontline-books.com, email info@frontline-books.com
or write to us at the above address.

TE WHARE WĀNANGA O TE ŪPOKO O TE IKA A MĀUI

VICTORIA
UNIVERSITY OF WELLINGTON

Published in New Zealand by Victoria University Press
PO Box 600, Wellington, New Zealand
www.victoria.ac.nz/vup

Published and distributed in the United States and Canada by the
Naval Institute Press
291 Wood Road, Annapolis, Maryland 21402-5034
www.nip.org

UK edition: ISBN 978-1-84832-5548
NZ edition: ISBN 978-0-86473-6192
US edition: ISBN 978-1-59114-7022

Publishing History
Report on Experience was originally published in 1947 by Oxford University
Press (OUP). It was reissued in 1967 by Blackwood & Janet Paul Limited,
Auckland, New Zealand, and in 1984 by OUP (New Zealand). This new edition
is the first to publish the original text in its entirety and contains new material
by M. R. D. Foot, Peter Whiteford and the author's son Richard Mulgan.

CIP data records for this title are available from the British Library,
the National Library of New Zealand and the Library of Congress.
Library of Congress Control Number 2009940376

Printed in Great Britain by MPG Books Limited

Contents

Preface

Richard Mulgan

Republication of John Mulgan's wartime memoir, *Report on Experience,* is most timely. With the death last year of Gabrielle, his widow and my mother, all those involved in the original revision and publication have now passed on. The book can be viewed more surely for what it is: a unique account of the British, and Europe, in the Second World War, from the perspective of one remarkably clear-sighted participant. Inclusion in the list of a major British publisher specialising in military and defence matters, with a foreword by the doyen of British military historians, Professor M. R. D. Foot, is a fitting destination for a book which has rarely received due recognition in the more than sixty years since it first appeared.

In the intervening period, the book has not been so much neglected, as read for reasons ancillary to its main purpose. The name of John Mulgan, though largely unknown in Britain, looms large in the much smaller world of New Zealand literature. His other book, a novel, *Man Alone*, published in 1939 and set in New Zealand, became a classic landmark in the development of New Zealand literature, much studied in schools and universities. More widely, Mulgan was seen as a member of a new generation of New Zealand writers in the 1930s who helped to develop a more nationalistic local literature, in keeping with the country's growing sense of cultural independence from the mother country.

From this perspective, the first chapter of *Report on Experience,* in which the author reflects on his New Zealand childhood and New Zealand society, has become an important historical source, both as contextual background for literary analysis of *Man Alone* and in New Zealand cultural history. His vivid word-pictures of the New Zealand landscapes echo those found in the novel. His idealised account of the New Zealand battalion, and of the superiority of New Zealand soldiers in comparison with their British counterparts, has boosted many New Zealanders' faltering self-esteem. These passages became the literary equivalent of All Black victories over rugby teams from the home nations (pp. 49–50). The striking words, 'and they marched into history' (p. 50) found their way onto several war memorials in the post-war period.

One happy by-product of the attention of literary critics has been that a scholar such as Associate Professor Peter Whiteford would find it worth while to devote his considerable editing skills to the task of restoring the original text of *Report on Experience.* As his careful introduction and footnotes make clear, the first edition was much amended in small, but not insignificant, ways by well-meaning hands, particularly Gabrielle's. Some major sections, critical of Mulgan's commanding officers, were also omitted. The original text can now be finally published in full, thanks to Whiteford's meticulous editing, a level of care that few wartime memoirs will have received.

But, in spite of the book's importance to New Zealanders, New Zealand itself, which the author had left in 1933 at the age of twenty-one and to which he never returned, is not the central focus of the book. New Zealand helps to anchor the author's independent perspective on the English, especially the English class system. But in doing so, it provides no distinctive viewpoint that has not been available to others who have left other similarly egalitarian, colonised societies, such as Ireland or Australia, to make their way in the metropolitan centre. The main attention is on the European war in general and the British army in particular.

Report on Experience has also been closely scrutinised for any clues it might yield about the author's death. Six weeks after posting the manuscript to Gabrielle in New Zealand, with the affectionate covering letter republished here (pp. 30–31), John Mulgan took his own life in a Cairo hotel. This decision, so shocking to his friends and so damaging to those who loved him, has continued to haunt his reputation. Reading the book in hindsight can certainly uncover an elegiac tone that suggests it may have been written as a deliberate testament and legacy. But this may be to confect wisdom after the event, a natural desire for personal and literary closure. There can be no conclusive judgment on either the reasons for his death or the role that this book played in it.

Republication after so many years offers a welcome chance to put this issue to one side. The nature of the author's death, so overwhelming to those who knew him, is quite marginal to the book's lasting quality. More important, perhaps, is the uncomplicated fact that he died. As with George Orwell, whose hard-headed progressive politics and deceptively plain literary style find many echoes in *Report on Experience*, early death serves to locate the voice more firmly in the period it described. The book speaks to us of how, in the war against fascism, individuals of humanity and honesty faced up to the terrible dilemmas that governments and political movements so blithely imposed upon them. At last, *Report on Experience* can come into its own, as an exceptionally perceptive and moving account of one man's war, and of war in general.

Canberra
September 2009

Foreword

M. R. D. Foot

Report on Experience is so vivid a book that its readers wish they could have met its author. I never did, though I may have passed him in the street—we were both living in Oxford for much of 1938–39, he at work at the University Press, I in my first year as an undergraduate. He had been born and brought up in New Zealand, and sent his wife and child there in 1941, by which time he was in the army. He had seen the world war coming, and joined his local territorial infantry regiment, the Oxfordshire and Buckinghamshire Light Infantry, with which he mobilised when uneasy peace gave way to phoney war. Over two years' garrison duty in Northern Ireland could hardly help but bore him; but he went with his battalion to the Egyptian desert, just in time to fight in both battles of El Alamein. He survived both, but quarrelled with his commanding officer, and escaped into special service, the Special Operations Executive, one of the nine British wartime secret services. He did not much care for parachuting, but nevertheless parachuted into Axis-occupied Greece, and had several months' hard work as a guerrilla behind enemy lines. After the Germans withdrew from

Greece, not much pursued by the communist-run half-bandit groups with which he tried to work, he was sent to Athens for the forlorn task of tidying up, trying to adjudicate amongst myriad claims to have helped in the secret war. Overwrought, he killed himself before he was thirty-five—leaving, rough-hewn, this unforgettable book.

One of the delights of the book lies in its style. He wrote in crystal-clear English, well seasoned with phrases from Shakespeare, Milton, Byron, Wordsworth, the King James version of the Bible; recollections from Aesop; ideas from Homer. There is never a sentence that needs re-reading to make its meaning plain. His thought was always enlightened—Voltaire, Condorcet, Diderot would have admired him, as he admired the life of reason that they stood for. He had completed his first degree at Auckland University College in New Zealand, and then read English at Merton College, Oxford at the knee of Edmund Blunden, the poet, so he was well taught as well as widely read.

He begins with an exile's evocation of New Zealand as a very old country, much older than its inhabitants, which is still working its magic on him from over ten thousand miles away; and then plunges into the maelstrom of European politics of the late 1930s, a subject worked over and over again by dons, diplomats and politicians ever since. What he has to say remains fresh, original and worth reflection; if we had had more John Mulgans, we might have had fewer world wars.

He skips over the boredom of garrison life, which can be intense, but criticises sharply two of the commanding officers, men promoted—presumably because it was Buggins's turn—to posts for which they were in his view wholly unfit. As he was adjutant to one, and second-in-command to the other, he was in a position to know. He was so outspoken that the Oxford University Press removed a few paragraphs by which the offenders could easily have been identified when they published the first edition in 1947; these are printed in this edition.

The vast distance between Mulgan and his wife was not abbreviated by the vagaries of wartime posts. Serving soldiers got no chances then to talk by intercontinental telephone. Those of them who were married had to keep in touch with their wives as best they could by letters, when they had time to write them, and these could seldom go all the way by air—they were often entrusted to ships, which were often sunk by enemy action. John and Gabrielle could not help slipping somewhat out of touch with each other; and some of his change of address notices went astray. She was still writing to him in Northern Ireland when he was serving in the Western Desert, and still writing to him in the desert when he was at a special service training school in Palestine. Once he went into Greece, she got a monthly typed note from a stranger in General Headquarters Cairo to say that he was well and sent his love—for about a year on end. She got no support from him when she most needed it—she fell dangerously ill, and lost a breast;

he got no support from her when he most needed it, because the necessities of secrecy buried him in the mountains of Thessaly, out of touch with everyone on his own side, except for a tenuous radio link with Cairo for orders and supplies. She did not even know, could not even know, which country he was in. These are unavoidable perils of secret war; she did not even know his war had gone secret, and he could not tell her.

It is all the more remarkable that he could summon the intellectual energy to draft out this book at all, writing in Athens just after the exertions of cross-examining claimants. Various rough spots in his typescript were ironed out by editors and sub-editors at OUP while they were preparing for press; this edition notes all of these changes, and the editor has done his best to restore the original.

Mulgan tried to fight in Greece alongside the Greek army of popular liberation, which was under covert communist control. He was quite lucky not to be unobtrusively bumped off by the communists, who regarded every officer in the British forces with profound class suspicion as a presumed enemy. He was able to perceive the dexterity of their propaganda, and the foundation of bloody-mindedness on which their incipient despotism rests: two determined men, one of whom is always awake, can between them control a village. He was thus amongst the earliest of the left-wing intelligentsia, outside the communist Soviet Union, to perceive that it was not after all the harbinger of paradise on Earth most of them had supposed, but a despotism like any other. The Greek communists were prepared to let him carry out some railway sabotage, which his own high command thought essential, in exchange for gold sovereigns and small arms, parachuted in intermittently.

One of the most telling passages recounts a talk with a village priest, who begged him as he was preparing a rail demolition to make sure that it did harm to the enemy commensurate with the burnings the Germans were sure to carry out in the village. He quotes, pretty well verbatim, a long talk he had with a fisherman from Euboea, who had travelled on foot thirteen times to Athens during the occupation, convoying men and messages, and never been caught but once (which had left him partly crippled). These pages bring out superbly the toughness of real resisters, the harrowing shortages of occupied life, and the unreal confidence of the Allied high command stationed in Cairo, which needed results and did not pause long enough to think of how they were to be secured on the spot.

He died the night of 25–26 April 1945: that is, a few days before Hitler's suicide brought the war in Europe to a close, and a few months before the first two nuclear bombs used in anger wound up the struggle with the Japanese and altered the nature of war between the great powers for ever.

But not all wars are fought by great powers against each other. A great many of the armed struggles since 1945 have been guerrilla conflicts, comparable to the war John Mulgan was fighting in Greece in 1943–44:

what happened to him then can count for a good deal now, in the current battlefields against terror and subversion. He was a subversive himself, and a highly deft one; that does not make what he did useless to today's security services.

What he did, and what he thought, as set out in the pages that follow, provide a fascinating set of examples of how a man can cope with difficulty and danger. Setting aside the abrupt way he chose to leave his life, there is a great deal here that is worth contemplating and copying.

Hertfordshire
August 2009

Introduction: the Textual History

Peter Whiteford

In March 1945, John Mulgan posted to his wife, Gabrielle, what he described in the accompanying letter as 'the draft and outline of a book I'd like to write'.[1] The book had been written in the preceding months while Mulgan was stationed in Athens, distributing money from the curiously named 'Liquidation Fund' to local people who had worked with the British Liaison Officers, or who had suffered reprisals as a result of activities of the partisans or the SOE.[2] The work he was engaged in, as Vincent O'Sullivan notes, was dispiriting work;[3] and there may be a more than literal sense in which he ends by describing himself as 'writing late at night in the darkened city of Athens'. By the middle of April, he had completed the assignment in Greece and was transferred back to Cairo, a city for which he had little affection; one week later, he

1 The letter is reproduced in the pages that follow.
2 Hence the rather sardonic pun in the letter Mulgan left at his death for Colonel Dolbey, which began with an apology for leaving 'this particular problem of liquidation on your hands'. Quoted in Vincent O'Sullivan, *Long Journey to the Border: A Life of John Mulgan* (Auckland: Penguin, 2003), p. 336.
3 *Long Journey to the Border*, p. 327.

was found dead in his hotel bed from an overdose of morphine, in the words of the inquest report 'taken intentionally by the deceased while the balance of his mind was disturbed'.[4] The typescript that he had sent to his wife, which he rather offhandedly described as neither well said nor clearly written, thus gained a special status, and seemed to demand publication; but it was thirty months before it was released by his former employer, Oxford University Press, in October of 1947.

The delay was not due to any reluctance on the part of OUP; Gabrielle Mulgan approached the Press when she returned to Oxford from New Zealand after the war, and both Kenneth Sisam and Geoffrey Cumberlege replied to her towards the end of 1945 conveying their very favourable response, and expressing a desire to publish the work.[5] Indeed, the original plan was to produce something rather more substantial, including photographs from Greece and New Zealand, and more elaborate maps than finally appeared. Eventually, the photographs had to be set aside, the available negatives not being of good enough quality, and only a single map was included (which caused 'no little trouble'[6] and was still being prepared

---

4   *Long Journey to the Border*, p. 339.
5   Correspondence relating to the publication of *Report* is preserved in a folder held in the Alexander Turnbull Library, Wellington, MS-Papers-7906-50. I am grateful to Richard Mulgan for permission to examine the restricted papers in the Mulgan collection. Unless otherwise noted, quotations in the following paragraphs are from letters in this folder.
6   So described by the OUP editor, David Ascoli, in a letter to Gabrielle

as late as May 1947) of the area within Greece where Mulgan had served. Two matters in particular, however, combined to hold up the publication.[7]

There was a strong desire on the part of all those involved to include a biographical note or memoir, expounding something of John Mulgan's life and character. Alan Mulgan, for example, wrote to Gabrielle at about this time describing the book as 'highly objective; it does not disclose the lighter, gayer side of John's character; and this [. . .] should be brought out in the foreword'.[8] Alan Mulgan had proposed seeking James Bertram's help with the foreword, an idea that appealed to Gabrielle because, as she acknowledged to Jack Bennett, 'I liked his notice of the novel in *Tomorrow*.' Bertram proved difficult to contact, however, and when he was finally reached was not keen on collaborating (so is unlikely to be the Oxford friend quoted at the conclusion of the foreword). Gabrielle also approached Geoffrey Cox (another close friend from Oxford), but he declined for reasons that were never made clear;[9] in the end, the memoir was written chiefly by Bennett and was completed in April 1946. It was warmly received by

---

Mulgan, in February, 1947.

7   In fact there were three, but the third could not be attributed to anything directly associated with the book. Coal shortages in 1947 forced ongoing problems with electricity generation, and printing presses were all affected by continued power cuts.

8   Quoted by Gabrielle Mulgan in a letter to J. A. W. Bennett. ATL MS-Papers-2377-17.

9   I am grateful to Richard Mulgan for drawing this to my attention (personal communication, 24 July 2009).

Mulgan's parents: prior to its publication, Alan wrote to David Ascoli that he felt 'Jack Bennett has done the introduction admirably, so well as to deepen the heart-ache'; and Marguerita wrote directly to Bennett in December 1948, thanking him for 'the fine way in which you wrote the personal memoir in John's book.' She went on to say 'there is no one I would rather have had do it and it must have been a difficult task. The tragedy of his death, the feeling that at the time had one of us been near it would not have happened, is so hard to accept that I have shirked very often bringing it to the surface. One goes on filling days with what has to be and adjusting oneself but the bitterness recurs.'[10]

Even more pressing, and more intractable, was the problem of what is variously referred to in the letters between Gabrielle and the Press as 'the Colonel episode' or 'the Colonel incident'. This refers to several severe and extended criticisms that Mulgan made about two of the officers under whom he served. The passages occur in Chapter Five and detail Mulgan's experiences with a battalion which he joined as its second-in-command just days before it left England. The first and third lieutenant-colonels under whom Mulgan served while with this battalion were both men whom he considered seriously, even dangerously, incompetent, and in his original script he made no bones about saying so. This naturally raised a difficulty in respect of the publication, for

10 Both letters are included in the folder of Bennett's papers. ATL MS-Papers-2377-17.

Mulgan's own rank and standing made identification of the officers a relatively simple matter (although he never names them). It was, as Kenneth Sisam wrote to Gabrielle, an 'unhappy complication'.

The correspondence makes clear that all those involved wished to retain what Mulgan had written, if it were possible to do so. In December 1945, Gabrielle wrote to Cumberlege: 'about the Colonel episode, I hope very much that you will feel able to risk leaving it as it stands. I should dislike to see it changed. It was a turning point in his life and for that reason is important.' It was indeed a turning point: Mulgan expressed his gravest concerns, first in a meeting with the second of the officers, and then formally in writing to 'higher authority'—which promptly accepted his resignation from the battalion. Ultimately, it was this course of action which led him to join the SOE and so took him to Greece. The Press was supportive of her wish—Cumberlege said he was 'perfectly willing to leave it provided it does not raise a question of libel'—but still thought it prudent to write to the War Office for an opinion. Early in January, Cumberlege wrote to her that he had received a letter from a Major Jepson with the news that the manuscript was 'regarded as not coming within the War Office jurisdiction for permission to publish'. Jepson further explained that 'censorship is now at an end', although he qualified his remarks by suggesting that 'if John had been living it might have been necessary to look through the book to see if there was anything by way of criticism of the army in general, or superior officers in particular'. Jepson's comments suggest that he may not in fact have seen Mulgan's text, but only been asked to offer a general opinion about the censorship of an officer's memoirs; for in addition to the very explicit criticisms of the two superior officers, there are also some acerbic remarks about other aspects of the British Army.

In spite of this assurance from the War Office (and perhaps bearing in mind Jepson's added caveat), Cumberlege was clearly still uneasy, and others who read and commented on the text included his predecessor as University Publisher, Sir Humphrey Milford, and another New Zealander, Dan Davin, who had taken Mulgan's place at the Press.[11] Cumberlege proposed showing it to Colonel Dolbey (although there is no evidence whether he did so or not) and he also took the precaution of sending the chapter to be read by the Press's solicitors. There is nothing extant in these papers that reports on any opinion offered by the solicitors, but it seems very likely that they advised against publication if the two officers were still alive, because of the dangers of libel.

Another who was consulted in the matter was Mulgan's old friend, Geoffrey Cox, and libel was

11 Vincent O'Sullivan has also told me that, in his conversations with Gabrielle and Paul Day, Freyberg was mentioned as one of those who advised against publication of the material. Lieutenant-General Sir Bernard Freyberg commanded the NZ Expeditionary Forces in Crete, North Africa, and Italy. If he was consulted, it is likely that it was Davin (who was one of Freyberg's senior intelligence officers) who sought his advice. However, Freyberg's name does not occur anywhere in the ATL material.

clearly in the forefront of his thinking. Although he had declined the invitation to write a memoir, he did offer an opinion on 'the Colonel incident' in a letter to Dan Davin (June 27 1946).[12] Cox agrees that 'the incident . . . is cardinal and must be preserved', but cautions against risking a libel suit. His letter proposes a number of deletions and substitutions, several of which Davin accepted, since they appear in the published text just as Cox recommended. Cox clearly regrets the editorial intervention, describing it as 'a tragedy that one should have to hammer and saw at the MS like this', but at the same time he remains confident that 'by the time the reader reaches this point he will already have a picture of John as an essentially fair and reasonable man, and so will feel that the colonel cannot have been anything but wrong'.

In August of that year, Davin wrote to Gabrielle telling her that 'both Colonels are still alive. So there seems nothing for it but to go ahead with the excisions', and he proposes to do it in draft (there is no mention of Cox's material) and then show it to her or to Jack Bennett. Thus it was that when *Report on Experience* was published, it included a very circumspect note from Bennett, saying merely that 'it has been necessary to delete a few references to persons still living'. In fact, the deletions were much more extensive than Bennett's note implies, and several

12 This material is taken from an unsigned copy of Cox's letter, written from his *News Chronicle* office in London. The copy is currently in private hands.

sections of the chapter were extensively rewritten. All the original material is restored in this edition.[13]

It would appear that the revision of Chapter Five was completed by October, when David Ascoli wrote to Gabrielle saying that he would 'recommend, in accordance with our conversation, that it should be left unpolished and untouched except for obvious matters of spelling and punctuation. It has already lost too much in the recasting of Chap. V and I do not feel that it should be submitted to any more surgery or remodelling.' The desire to retain as much as possible of the original was something that was shared by all.

One other who read the book prior to its publication was C. M. (Monty) Woodhouse. A letter exists from Woodhouse to Alan Mulgan (June 1947) in which the former acknowledges having just read the script which he found 'deeply moving'; he goes on to say that he has 'many times tried to put into writing my own feelings about Greece' but that 'John has made the task harder by doing it almost perfectly himself'. He continues, in a way that echoes Gabrielle's own preference, and the preferences of those at OUP, saying, 'I am glad his book is to be published exactly as he wrote it. It is too good to bear polishing.'[14]

In spite of those widely expressed wishes, there was rather more 'polishing' than merely spelling and punctuation. It is not possible now to determine who

13   Extracts from the material excised from Chapter Five have been quoted before, by Paul Day in his 1968 book on Mulgan in the Twayne series, and by O'Sullivan in his biography.

14   I am grateful to Vincent O'Sullivan for allowing me to see this letter, which is still in private hands.

was responsible for effecting the changes: Gabrielle Mulgan, Dan Davin, Jack Bennett and David Ascoli all contributed to the final form, but on significant matters it appears that Gabrielle had a key role. Apart from the extensive revision of Chapter Five and the standard copy editing to correct and normalize spelling and punctuation, there has been some touching up of points of grammar and usage and some polishing of style. Undoubtedly some of those changes bring about improvements, and it seems likely that Mulgan (an experienced editor himself) would have agreed to them had they been drawn to his attention; but in the text that is presented here I have restored what is in the original typescript if that can be defended.

One or two examples of the kind of changes effected may be noted here. On three or four occasions—in a memoir otherwise written in a very direct first person—Mulgan prefers a rather clumsy construction in which he uses an old-fashioned description of himself as 'the author' (see footnotes 9, 25, 49, 56). The awkwardness cries out for an editorial pen, and it is no surprise that someone changed the text. But it is worth noting, nevertheless, that at certain moments in his narrative this typically direct writer chose to distance himself from his material in these rather uncomfortable circumlocutions. More amusing is the somewhat pedantic alteration of Mulgan's 'thatched shepherd's hut' to 'shepherd's thatched hut'—no doubt technically more accurate in its observation of rules of proximity for attributive adjectives, but scarcely necessary to resolve any possible misunderstanding.

Beyond the far-reaching revisions of Chapter Five, the motives for which are generally clear enough, there remain a few alterations the rationale for which is not so obvious. Towards the end of Chapter One there are two beautifully written paragraphs in praise of the New Zealanders of the desert. Mulgan is clearly deeply impressed by those he meets, even surmising that 'to have produced these men for this one time would be New Zealand's destiny'. He admires in them 'good sense, patience, the versatility of practical men'. And he concludes the paragraph: 'They were volunteers, not mercenaries, and they marched into history.' When it was published, the first five words were deleted. A pencilled note (the hand appears to be Gabrielle's) in the archive asks, 'Were all the NZers volunteers?' Nothing else appears that relates to the excision, leaving open the question whether the sentence as Mulgan wrote it was felt to be technically inaccurate, or whether the word 'mercenaries' had caused some offence. Later, when Mulgan writes of the Italian surrender in Greece, he describes one Italian officer, commander of the Pinerolo division, as having 'political ambitions [which] he afterwards realized, since he managed to leave his men in Greece and make his way back to Italy'. In the published edition, any sense that the officer might have abandoned his men is removed, although it seems clear that, accurate or not, that was how Mulgan interpreted his actions. Finally, there seems a rather nice irony in the decision to delete the overt reference to the Ministry of Economic Warfare, and allow just a neutral reference to 'the Ministry'. Presumably some sense of security motivated this deletion, but as Michael Foot has noted, the MEW was itself the cover: 'Members of SOE could tell their friends they worked for MEW; that was only cover.'[15]

The footnotes record substantive changes that were introduced in the first edition, including some instances of error introduced at the editorial stage, but I have not recorded all the corrections of spelling and punctuation made to what was, after all, an unrevised typescript. The footnotes also record some literary allusions that occur in *Report*, for one of the surprising things about the text is the noticeable literariness of its opening chapters. There are references here to Shakespeare and the Bible, and to Wordsworth, Longfellow, Horace, Lenin, Montague, and Mulgan's much-loved Housman. Interestingly, there are also echoes of Cox's *Defence of Madrid*, but that may be a result of their shared journalistic activities. O'Sullivan has noted the sombre model of Gibbon's *Decline and Fall* (a work Mulgan returned to often and read during his time in Greece); equally, the borrowings from Housman and Longfellow strike a note that is sometimes nostalgic, sometimes elegiac, so that throughout the early chapters in particular there is a constant mood of loss and of longing. But if there is some nostalgia in the glance back to New

15 M. R. D. Foot, *SOE. The Special Operations Executive 1940–1946* (Pimlico, 1984), p. 35.

Zealand, there is a realism in much of the book that is both hard-headed and hard-won. It is, as the title so clearly affirms, the product of experience.

Not that the title we now have is Mulgan's: that too was changed.[16] According to his letter to Gabrielle, the work was to be called 'Summary of Experience'; the alternative *Report on Experience* was suggested early on, perhaps by Bennett, and preferred by Sisam and Cumberlege, so that eventually Gabrielle agreed to the change. Mulgan might not have minded too much, for it continues the habit of literary allusion, this time borrowing the title of a poem by Mulgan's Oxford tutor, Edmund Blunden. The correspondents from the Press insisted that the new title was more accurate, that it better conveyed the content; but there is equally some commercial reality in their opinion that it was easier to ask for in a bookshop. That, too, is something of which Mulgan might well have approved. One might choose to disagree with the assertion that the new title is more accurate—as a report, it seems remarkably lacking in detail, but offers instead a careful distillation or summary of experience—but it would not be possible now to replace the title by which it has been known for over sixty years. What is possible though, now, is to allow the experience that it records its own uncensored voice.

Wellington
July 2009

---

16   Ironically, so too was the title of his major published work, the novel *Man Alone*, which he proposed to call 'Talking of War'.

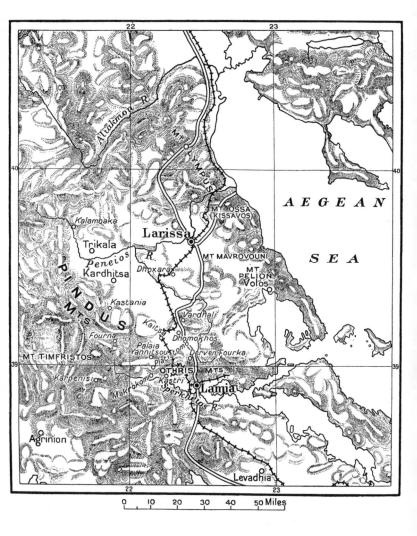

Map of Thessaly and the Pindus Mountains,
reproduced from the first edition.

15 March 1945

Dearest Gabrielle,

You asked me a long time ago to send you what I had
been writing and I'm afraid I didn't. I'm sending you
this now, in case I'm longer coming home than I hope,
since I thought it might amuse you and perhaps you
could type it for me. An odd little Greek typed the
first part—he wanted to improve his English, though
I doubt he took the best model for that. It isn't a
book, but only the draft and outline of a book I'd
like to write. I destroyed I'm afraid more than there
is here and don't like much what there is but thought
it best to finish off in outline and however short, the
form of a book, since the habit of not writing grows
on one. So I've written it down and if I had to publish
it now, would call it 'Summary of Experience', which
is what it is. It has in it all the little that I've thought
over this war and the peace that we're now coming to.
It isn't as well said or as clearly written as it should
be, and would need elaboration to be convincing. I
think every man writes in the end just as much as
he has in him to say, and I long ago realised that the
little talent I have lacked inventiveness and wouldn't
bear more than a certain strain being laid upon it.
The fact that one has deep convictions about people
and society and the way the world should be made
to exist for us, doesn't mean that one can write a
good book. What small virtues I have, some of them

sadly cultivated with rather painful experience, are practical and don't lead to literature, or at least all the literature they've so far led to could be wrapped up in this small package I'm sending you now. However, I promise you sweetheart, if I ever do publish a book which I could be in any way proud of, I'll dedicate it to you—strictly against the rules we used to lay down for authors in the Press—as a slight gesture of thanks, and love, for all that you suffered from me in my younger and less sensible days.

I seem to be getting unnecessarily solemn and declamatory on this typewriter, it comes of writing late at night in the darkened city of Athens, so will just send you now my love—not in a dedication—and for Richard, the schoolboy, bless him,

John

Report on Experience

Chapter One

It seems a long time ago now since I was young in New Zealand. No ordinary man wants to write about himself in the sense that he thinks his life important; but if one has something to set down that concerns the world that we know now, it can only grow out of a background and certain accidents and events that have happened to the man who is writing. And it is as well, therefore, to write about these things clearly and honestly, without exaggerating the value of individual experiences. Everything that happened to me in the peace between the wars, and in the war itself, produced in me no more than a feeling, for which I am grateful now, of being part of a community who lived through the same times, had the same fears, and held to the same beliefs.

New Zealand is a fine small country. I believe it still is, though it is a long time since I saw anything of it and only recapture the country occasionally now from people who have been there more recently. Wordsworth believed that communion with wild and natural things takes us back to God or re-establishes for us the pattern of some former ideal life. This always seemed to me a pleasant and harmless philosophy, but I reckoned it was probably untrue. A materialist by nature, I distrusted all attempts to dispose of the only kind of life that I know, the immediate and present world that I see every morning and like. Something obtuse in my character made me side with Dr. Johnson—as against Bishop Berkeley— and believe that other men probably see much the same world too—whether they like it or not. There was a deep and elemental truth in the Wordsworth doctrine, nevertheless. Even though the vision of his belief was denied to me, I came in the end to know that much of what he wrote was true, and that, in particular, the land and the people whom we know when we are young stay with us and haunt us until we die. I don't know that this proves anything about immortality or reincarnation, but it is a fact. If you try to fight against this truth, and forget the country of your youth, as I did for a long time, you will lose the fight and wither internally of homesickness.

For New Zealand is a good country. It has the feeling of being a very old country, though not at all in the European sense where countries are old with the marks of humanity. A country like England is smooth and rounded with the passing of unnumbered generations. It bears the lines of long-forgotten ploughing, old stones and buildings, and the neglected tracks of men. Along the misty valleys lies coldly the reminder that all is ashes under Uricon.[1]

1   The phrase 'ashes under Uricon' occurs at the end of A. E. Housman's 'On Wenlock Edge', No. XXXI in *A Shropshire Lad*

New Zealand is very old, much older than any of this, and quite untouched by men. Its rocks and mountains are worn smooth by south Pacific winds. They are very cold to touch and very clean. The country, with its sharp hills, gives you the same feeling as the clear salt of the sea. The country is, in fact, so old in itself that none of us have dared to touch it; we have only just begun to live there. The Maoris who came before us moved among the dark heavy trees like ghosts and could have sailed away at any time and never left a mark. We could leave it ourselves now: in a few years the red-roofed wooden bungalows would rot with borer and crumble into the earth. Fern would cover the grassland and, after fern, small trees would come and in time the dark, rich, matted bush again. Other men might come in a hundred years and nothing that we had left would worry them, but they could draw strength as we have done from the sharp, fierce lines of the hills and the streams always running and the wide sea on every side.

This has been another cause of conflict to New Zealanders, that there have never been enough of them nor have they had sufficient confidence in themselves to take over the country, so that they live there like strangers or as men might in a dream which will one day wake and destroy them.

There is nothing soft about New Zealand, the country. It is very hard and sinewy, and will outlast many of those who try to alter it.

(1896). On Mulgan's fondness for Housman's verse, see O'Sullivan, *Long Journey to the Border*, pp. 70, 113.

This is one reason why New Zealanders, a young people but already with a place in history, are often wanderers and restless and unhappy men. They come from the most beautiful country in the world, but it is a small country and very remote. After a while this isolation oppresses them and they go abroad. They roam the world looking not for adventure but for satisfaction. They run service cars in Iraq, or[2] gold-mines in Nevada, or newspapers in Fleet St. They are a queer, lost, eccentric, pervading people who will seldom admit to the deep desire that is in all of them to go home and live quietly in New Zealand again.

Those who do not go abroad and do not travel are afflicted with the same sad restlessness. They are all the time wanting to set out across the wide seas that surround them in order to find the rest of the world. When we went sailing, we used to head out into the Hauraki Gulf from Auckland. This is a wide gulf, locked in by islands so that it has a sense of harbour and refuge and security. Inside the gulf and the harbours, there are tidal creeks and shoal beaches. But when you reach the outside of the gulf you come to an ocean, and here the beaches are of white, wind-driven sand, covered with driftwood from all the Pacific seas. A long, deep, and monotonous swell rides in at the end of a long journey. New Zealanders are all the time standing on the edge of these seas. They spend their lives wanting to set out across the wide oceans that surround them in order to find the rest of the world.

2   or] omitted in 1st edn.

One way and another, those who are going and those who are staying have all the time within them this sad inner conflict and frustration. This is the first fact to remember about New Zealanders, who live in the most beautiful country of the world.

You can guess, nevertheless, that we had a fairly good time there when we were young, when we were young enough not to worry about our place in the world or what was happening outside us. No one is really happy when he is young. You try to do too much and to be too many things with too many different people. Later on, when a man gets older, he begins to understand that he hasn't any human right to absolute happiness, and he is content with particular and limited forms of satisfaction. But for a place to grow up in, putting aside the disabilities of youth, New Zealand was better than most.

The two islands of New Zealand run a thousand miles from one end to the other[3] and something under two million people share the whole of this land. They don't share it altogether equitably, but there seemed to be plenty of room for everybody, and the sea and the air and a good deal of the land itself was free. We had no sense of poverty about us in those days. When I grew older and knew a little more, I was shocked to find that there had been poor people in New Zealand. In the depression, odd and ugly facts came up to meet us. But they were foreign to the atmosphere in which we had lived and I think most people felt them to be so.

3   to the other] typescript has 'to another'.

Everyone in New Zealand went to the same schools and learned the same things, and this gave us a common basis for any conversations we cared to have. Boys shared the same accent which I remember being told was neither beautiful nor standard English, but I like hearing it now when I meet it. On the whole nobody talked very much, certainly not more than they needed to. Nobody went about practising conversation as a fine art—at least not in the circles I mixed with as a young man.

We were a naive society and I suppose a little crude. Every now and again some Englishman, such as[4] a university professor or visiting lecturer, would land and deplore to the first journalist he met—we had newspapers—the lack of culture in our midst. Then someone who worried about these things—we had cultured men too—would write to the paper and say, 'This is not so, stranger,' or words to that effect, and quote him[5] the example of some one of our young men who might recently have written a book or painted a picture. For a few days, there would be a politely heated correspondence in the press, and after that it would die down again until the next educated Englishman arrived. The bulk and generality of New Zealanders cared little for these things. They were, perhaps, a little uneasy when one of these visitors was about, and very defensive. New Zealanders never liked having their deficiencies pointed out to them—who does? They never tried to glory in their

4   such as] typescript has 'like'.
5   him] omitted in 1st edn.

lack of culture, but I don't think they really minded not having any.

Our main pursuits were only cultural in the broadest sense. They were horse-racing, playing Rugby football, and beer-drinking—especially playing football. There were other minor interests like yachting, mountaineering, politics. Religious meetings of a faith-healing kind had a considerable following; faith-healers never lacked an audience. A simple people, after all, to whom much poetry was denied, the New Zealanders took their romance in the form of bucket-shops, gold-bricks, and companies who claimed to make petrol out of water. Gentle grafters who could raise the fare from Sydney or San Francisco praised our simplicity and treated New Zealand as a holiday ground.

Rugby football was the best of all our pleasures: it was religion and desire and fulfilment all in one. Most New Zealanders can look back on some game which they played to win and whose issues seemed to them then a good deal more important than a lot that has happened since. This phenomenon is greatly deprecated by a lot of thinkers who feel that an exaggerated attention to games gives the young a wrong sense of values. This may well be true, and if it is true, the majority of New Zealanders have a wrong sense of values for the whole of their lives. But to be frank, and since we live in a hard world, and one that has certainly not in my time got any softer, I found in wartime that there was a considerable virtue in men who had played games like professionals to win, and not, like public-school boys and amateurs, for exercise. So that perhaps it would be more correct to say that the virtues and values of the New Zealanders were not so much wrong as primitive, and to this extent useful in the current collapse of civilization.

New Zealanders, when they went to war, found it easier to get down to the moral plane of a German soldier, and were even capable of thinking a ruse or two ahead in the game of total war. Englishmen spent some time and casualties in finding war ungentlemanly before they tossed the rules overboard and moved in on the same basis. I don't know that the cunning and professionalism of my fellow countrymen is to be commended on abstract grounds, but these are comfortable qualities to have about in wartime. Oddly enough I don't think these things affected their natural kindliness, nor the kind of ethics that they expect from people in private life. It was only that they looked on war as a game, and a game to New Zealanders is something that they play to win, against the other side and the referee, if necessary. Personally I still prefer games that way and find them more interesting.

It wasn't always the football season in New Zealand. After winter the sun came in. In the sun the fern hills grew very brown and the clay roads yellow with dust. The deep green of the bush in the mountains never changed but a blue mist came over them. Out to sea the gulf islands looked very friendly.

Winter and summer, the New Zealanders were fairly happy. I don't know that they were more happy in any absolute sense than Greek peasants or Czech factory workers, but they were physically very well, which gave them a start. They moved in a good world and knew it and liked it. In the times about which I'm writing now, in the peace and prosperity years between the end of the First World War and the great depression, nothing appeared to be wrong with the world as we saw it from New Zealand. The only troubles that people had were personal and domestic.

I know that personal and domestic troubles can hurt as deeply as any other kind of ill-fortune; but there is this difference in them that a man feels them all the time as being subject to his personal endeavour. He understands them as being due to some human agency and though he may not find the solution, he knows that the solution is also personal and domestic.

It would be a mistake to look back and say that those were the good days, those golden twenties when the sun was shining. They were the dumb, unconscious days, in a world of our boyhood that will never return to us again. But the thoughts of youth are long, long thoughts[6] and those years seem to have expanded now until they fill a larger place than they deserve. It is also clear to me now that not only our youth made those years golden. They were easy years, and after they passed, from the time of the depression onwards, we were caught up in events that never allowed us to

6   Mulgan alludes here to the refrain from Longfellow's 'My Lost Youth'.

move with the same sense of freedom that we had then.

The shadow of depression ended this golden summer. 1929 was the last of the good years. In 1930 we were brave and courageous and beginning to wonder how we might earn a living when we left college and started work. In 1931 everyone was still talking about the depression as if it was a rainstorm that would blow over and leave the earth green and smiling and fresher than it had been before. Towards the end of 1931, the bottom dropped out of the markets that supported us. After that people spoke about the depression as something rather more than a rainstorm, as a national calamity that had begun to affect their lives.

Trouble on a large scale in this way was something new to us. I suppose there had been bad times before in the pioneer days. The Great War was no picnic—though commercially profitable to the farmers, a time for death rather than for bankruptcy. But the depression was something very big and overwhelming and intangible. People resented it, not only because it did them harm but because they couldn't understand it. It settled on New Zealand like a new and unwanted stranger, a grey and ghastly visitor to the house.

I don't think, retrospectively, that we reacted very well towards the new arrival. It was a source of grief to many New Zealanders to find their spiritual resources in quality well below their sunburnt and muscular bodies. Home-brewed beer and pamphlets on Douglas credit[7] were standard panaceas in the sombre winter of 1932. The search for a short cut, the easy road home, the quick cure, the patent medicine, was feverish, bitter, and unsuccessful.

It is not easy now to explain this sudden and bleak change in our lives. We had lived as a community in a fair state of material happiness and unconcern, and now the insubstantial nature of this living came home to us. It was emphasized by hungry men who threw rocks at shop-windows and by an underlying hatred in the eyes of relief workers on the roads.

Economists had the status of witch-doctors in those days; but their panaceas were less satisfactory. The position of a primary-producing country, they told us, is not altogether equitable. (We were a primary-producing country, though few of us used the long word for it. We sold wool and butter and frozen meat on a British market and prices fell with the British pound.) Prices of primary products, the economists said, tend to fall first and to fall farthest. It seemed, moreover, that they took longer to rise again. We lived on the end of a pendulum swung by a trade cycle that no one had bothered to assess before, and now that we came to recognize its existence, there didn't seem much possibility of our controlling the trade cycle from our remote end of the pendulum.

Certain changes came over New Zealand at this

7 The phrase refers both to the monetary theories of the reformist, H. C. Douglas, and to the Australian political party that took his name. Douglas had visited New Zealand about the time of which Mulgan is writing.

time. We were young then and sensitive to these
changes and minded them disproportionately. It was
noticeable that men stopped speaking openly to one
another, and the majority favoured a doctrine that
every man's duty was to look after himself. This, of
course, was the fine old flavour of the pioneers and of
rugged, economic liberalism, but I think, from what
I have read, that the pioneers turned out to help their
neighbours in distress, and survived because they
lived as a community, and not as men alone.

Altogether there was not very much satisfaction to
be got from these changes. The sun shone less warmly
in the crisis period of 1931-1932, the drinking was less
spontaneous, and even the Rugby football suffered in
quality.

In Auckland the smooth suburban gardens sloped
down to the sea. Here in the carefully tended parks of
Remuera lived the aristocracy. Their daughters were
lovely and satirical, drinking surreptitious gin in the
half-empty cabarets. The homes of the town workers
ate wide into the country, red-roofed, with their small
gardens, concrete paths, and modern sanitation. The
red-and-yellow 'trams de luxe' carried them clanging
to their work, some of them in this period a little
less regularly to work. They were nervous then,
expressions a trifle compressed, eyes more harassed.
Beyond that,[8] roads and railways opened into country
that was still new and workable, northwards into clay
and fern, dead forests, warm valleys; southwards into
dairy country where the cows moved factory-like to

8   that] omitted in 1st edn.

the milking-sheds. Here, there were men working who had lost their old belief in a gradual possession of their land. Their wives and children rose at dawn to the rancour of milking machines. Southward again was bush country, half-claimed and still unwon, hills burnt and no grass sown, valleys of lonely settlement.

There was food in New Zealand at this time, but the trains did not always load it. Rain fell that winter on empty docks. Did we hear, perhaps for the first time, the voice of a people that has recognized an injustice, that has perceived the possibility of disorganization in its midst? Economists and old men told us that all this had happened before and would pass away, but this comfort was of philosophic form and our natures were sensuous and unsuited to philosophy.

First-hand knowledge is lacking to this author[9] of the successive stratagems that were adopted by the country of which he writes[10] to avoid the ill-starred necessities of its position on the pendulum. I know that there was a change of government. It seems to have been a general rule that governments who encountered the depression went under for rather more than a political decade. The depression brought Hitler and Stanley Baldwin into power; it also gave the world Roosevelt, and a genial Liberal–Labour government in New Zealand. But I think the world lost out on balance. What happened in New Zealand

9   to this author] 1st edn. revises to 'to me'.
10   were adopted . . . he writes] 1st edn. revises to 'New Zealand adopted'.

depends on how you like your politics. Some say that an era of stringent economy and planless derision passed with acclamation into a period of benevolent revolution: others, from a different angle, that sound finance gave way to a wilderness of inflation, Douglas credit, State control—and even Socialism. At all events the pendulum moved up again and carried with it Hitler, Mr. Roosevelt, Stanley Baldwin, and many another. Passengers dropped by the way were the Negus of Abyssinia, several million Chinese, and the Spanish people. I am told on good authority that beer and horse-racing remained in favour in New Zealand. There were hot summers, and some very debatable football.

All this happened a long time ago and New Zealand is a far country, now, while I am writing this. It is distant not only on the other side of the world at war, but also distant in time. If I am remembering anything, it is not only of people that I care for and remember and hope some day to see again, but also of places and a peculiar memory of scent and light and sound that is the tide coming in at early morning at Manganese Point, or the surf at evening by Whatipu, or a bush river in flood somewhere north of Karamea. I know that if I went back now none of these things would seem the same, and the country would be different and full of a new lot of people. But there is no harm nor any difficulty in remembering.

Afterwards, a long time afterwards, I met the New Zealanders again, in the desert below Ruweisat ridge, the summer of 1942. It was like coming home.

They carried New Zealand with them across the sands of Libya. This was the division that had saved the campaign of 1941 at Sidi Rezegh. The next year, when Rommel came into Egypt, the same division drove down from Syria and up along the coast road against the tide of a retreating army to meet him, and waited for him at[11] Mersah Matruh. They held there for three days. By the evening of the third day, the whole Afrika Corps had lapped round them and was closing in. Ordered to come out, the New Zealanders attacked by night, led out their transport through the gaps they cleared, boarded it, and drove back to Alamein. Through all the days of that[12] hot and panic-stricken July they fought Rommel to a standstill in a series of attacks along Ruweisat ridge. They helped to save Egypt, and led the break-through at Alamein to turn the war.

They were mature men, these New Zealanders of the desert, quiet and shrewd and sceptical. They had none of the tired patience of the Englishman, nor that automatic discipline that never questions orders to see if they make sense. Moving in a body, detached from their homeland, they remained quiet and aloof and self-contained. They had confidence in themselves, such as New Zealanders rarely have, knowing themselves as good as the best the world could bring against them, like a football team in a more deadly game, coherent, practical, successful.

It seemed to me, meeting them again, friends grown

11   at] 1st edn. has 'near'.
12   that] 1st edn. has 'a'.

a little older, more self-assured, hearing again those soft, inflected voices, the repetitions of slow, drawling slang, that perhaps to have produced these men for this one time would be New Zealand's destiny. Everything that was good from that small, remote country had gone into them—sunshine and strength, good sense, patience, the versatility of practical men. They were volunteers, not mercenaries,[13] and they marched into history.

If the old world ends now with this war, as well it may, I have had visions and dreamed dreams[14] of another New Zealand that might grow into the future on the foundations of the old. This country would have more people to share it. They would be hard-working peasants from Europe that know good land, craftsmen that love making things with their own hands, and all men who want the freedom that comes from an ordered, just community. There would be more children in the sands and sunshine, more small farms, gardens, and cottages. Girls would wear bright dresses, men would talk quietly together. Few would be rich, none would be poor. They would fill the land and make it a nation.

In this country in a dreamed-of future, men will remember names of desert places that have been dignified by fighting, battle honours of a small country, of that New Zealand of the past, and they will share these things as part of a history that will be dear to them. 'All earth has witnessed that they

13 They were volunteers, not mercenaries,] omitted in 1st edn.
14 See Joel 3: 1 and Acts 2: 16.

answered as befitted their ancestry; that they endured as the strong influences about their youth taught them to endure.'[15]

15 The quotation is taken from a speech of Rudyard Kipling, 'The Scot and the War', delivered at Edinburgh University in 1920, and published in *A Book of Words* (1928).

Chapter Two

Close ties bound the New Zealanders to England. If the form that clothed these ties was sentiment and tradition, their content and reality was economic dependence and the fact that we were a small country with no nationality of our own. New Zealanders are not given to abstract thinking nor to the formulation of principles. They have never questioned the unity that joins them to England. This same unity has taken them overseas twice in the last generation to correct the errors of someone else's foreign policy. The kind of loyalty that New Zealanders possess is stupid, irrational, and, in some melancholy way, satisfying to the heart. It has the texture of family relationships that can be full of internal bitterness but united against the outside world, that can be relied upon beyond ordinary friendships[16] in times of sickness and death.

We are growing up now, nevertheless, and may be permitted to speak objectively of our parents. We can dispense now with the legend which tradition fostered for us of a benign England, the staid old mother of

16   friendships] 1st edn. has 'friendship'.

the seven seas. I don't know whether this England of our story books ever existed. It was a country, as I remember it, of rounded, lovely hills, its slate-roofed villages rich in history. In this faery England the aristocracy were patriarchal and humane. Men worked on the land for love as well as profit, and played cricket in the long summer evenings. Rose-cheeked children went happily to the village school.

No one told us that in England the villages had died, that farming had ceased to be an occupation for men and had become an expensive hobby for gentlemen. None of the books explained that in England men spoke different languages, that the well-to-do had given up the accents of their counties and adopted the accents of a class.

England was Tilbury on a raw November morning, streets of tenement houses crowded with pale, flat-capped working men who obviously had no work. England was wide-ribboned roads littered with facile, emotionless suburbs, a country-side ravaged by charabanc parties, old buildings and memorials commercialized into quaintness.

Within the borders of this despoiled country moved that great race who must be free or die.[17] A caste system more rigid than the Hindu divided them by dress, occupation, and accent. Two[18] million men

17 From Wordsworth's description of the English people, in 'It is not to be thought of'.
18 Two] Mulgan's typescript originally read 'Two', but he has crossed this out, and has 'Ten' in the margin. The 1st edn. reverts to 'Two': the number on 'the dole' was nowhere near ten million in the period of which he writes.

and women queued patiently for labour or the dole.
From their eyes had gone the last gleam of resistance
and left only a tired endurance. Another ten millions,
the central core,[19] bowler-hatted, white-collared,
moved in a rhythm whose every motive played for
safety.[20] These were the people who swayed the vote.
Their fears and prejudices, easily predictable, were
the playground of politicians. And, travelling first-
class in sealed compartments, were the men who
got things done, the wise fellows, the professionals,
the self-selected. Their distinguishing mark was an
ignorance, neither affected nor concealed, of their
fellow men.

The life of a German diplomat is a hard one, and
I think we can now afford to extend a little sympathy
to Ribbentrop, who wrote the English off as decadent.
All the evidence favoured his judgement. None of his
English friends corrected him.

After 1931, the English Left went underground.
They gave up thoughts of political power, and
embraced that sad pessimism which is the heritage
of all radical thought. The middle classes took over
power but wanted neither decision nor control. They
were happiest when allowed to avoid those issues
which destiny prepares for great empires. Only rarely
did they show emotion or interest. They permitted
themselves a certain grave excitement in 1926 and
again in 1931 when told their savings were in jeopardy.

19   Another . . . core] 1st edn. revises to 'Ten millions of the rest'.
20   a rhythm . . . safety] 1st edn. revises to 'monotonous rhythm and
     played for safety at every turn'.

In 1935 political jobbery over Abyssinia was a little too flagrant for that Nonconformist conscience which in better days voted for Gladstone, and, in our time, for Baldwin. There was a brief flicker of emotion, enough to unseat Lord Templewood, brief enough to welcome him back to the government within six months. Ah, most wicked speed to post with such dexterity[21]—his place and punishment in history is at least secure, an enduring connotation with Laval.[22] And in 1936 there was an abdication issue which men and women took to heart and wrestled with, like a family problem, while Madrid entered on the first of its four sombre winters. Berchtesgaden and Munich in 1938[23] were myths made to order for the English middle classes—'Business man with umbrella defies modern giant, Returns with magic piece of paper, All live happily in golden age.'

None of this would bear recalling now if we

---

21 See Hamlet I. ii. 156-57.
22 Samuel Hoare (1st Viscount Templewood) was Foreign Minister at the time of the Italian invasion of Abyssinia. With his French equivalent, Pierre Laval, he devised a plan that would call a halt to the war by allowing Italy to retain most of Abyssinia. Public outcry led to his resignation, although he was re-instated some months later. In one of the notes in ATL MS-Papers-7906-50 Gabrielle Mulgan proposes reverting to 'Samuel Hoare', since Templewood did not have his title at the time. She also appears to have had some concern about the comment; in another note, she writes 'Lord Templewood – libel?'
23 The locations of two of Chamberlain's meetings with Hitler, where Hitler's demands in respect of the Sudetenland were formally discussed. Chamberlain resisted those demands at Berchtesgaden, but later he and the French prime minister, Edouard Daladier, signed the Munich Agreement transferring the area to Germany.

could be sure it would never happen again. Who could predict that these same people would face the terror of 1940 with courage and delight, and be prepared to fight on and many of them to die in all the loneliness of that time? The pride that grew from the bombed cities of England had within it an element of expiation, the pride of a people that had watched in silence, strangled and hushed by their leaders, the endurance of Madrid and Barcelona, Shanghai and Chungking, and Warsaw,[24] and could now share as veterans in their own right the same communion of suffering.

This, at least, was the comment of an American in 1940 who added, talking in his remote and friendly way, that regrettably the bombs falling each night on London did not always fall on the right people. Of course, he said, a war where the bombs fell only on the deserving would take rather more organization than we possess at present.

It was the same American who, standing one morning by the smoking ruins of the Temple and watching the Londoners pass soberly to work, was moved to shout, 'Get angry, you dumb bloody souls, get angry', and drew on himself only the unwinking stare of a people traditionally tolerant of eccentricity among foreigners.

The English are a very great people, and this author for one is[25] proud to have been with them during this war. They have virtues of patience and sanity in time

24 and Warsaw] omitted in 1st edn.
25 this author for one is] 1st edn. revises to 'I for one am'.

of crisis, and they always win the last battle. But they cut things rather fine in 1940, and another time it might be preferable to win some battles before the last or perhaps prevent the war from starting at all.

But lament, then, for the sad, chaotic logic of those years. For it was clear enough what each would do, how one would rearm the enemy for profits in cash, another hold back from opposing him for fear of endangering the sacred traditions of property, yet a third refuse to provide defences for fear of the two-edged weapons that his native opponents might obtain, a fourth grow pacifist from abhorrence of the facts of the war. The trend of the world was plain, inexorable, destined for calamity.

Fear, not of death but of an unknown horror, overshadowed men's minds. In the dark magnitude of London this fear was ever present. The twisted streets of Pimlico and mournful, ever-weeping Paddington lay open to the night-bomber. Mr. Baldwin and Mr. Gilbert Murray[26] spoke in earnest agreement on this one fact. Politicians offered fear without hope, counselled patience without remedy, and you could feel running in the muddied current of the London stream, in the restless, not yet stampeding herd, the fears and aspirations of the blind, of the dark unciphered millions who no longer possessed the

26 Gilbert Murray was a prominent British classicist, and Regius Professor of Greek at Oxford University from 1908-1936. He was also very involved with the Liberal Party, and closely involved with the League of Nations, including as an organiser of the 'Peace Ballot' of 1934-35.

present, and[27] awaited with Anglo-Saxon foreboding the long, hopeless future.

To the black-coated millions in tubeways returning, what answer, news-vendor, what answer? No war to-day, madam, no war to-day. One more warless day, one more day for the tubes to run smoothly homewards.

This England is a fine country, or was, or will be again. But in those years she gave no comfort to her lovers, and many a lover thought longingly of escape. It's not done to leave a sinking ship, someone was saying, but a different matter when the captain scuttles it. In the end the lovers stayed, for there was no life for them, as they knew, without England, nor any ultimate escape from the issues of a war that concerned all men.

The years and events rolled faster towards the close. Talking with journalists, the bloodshot-eyed and cynical, in dark Johnsonian taverns, fresh back from Europe, from *Anschluss,* partition, nationalist *risorgimento*—like talking to explorers sunburnt from darkest Africa in the darker eighties. Plotting with mild detached interest the arrows of penetration on the map, intelligence officer for the democracies. You have the staff plan, sir? No, not actually the plan. The command have not yet entrusted me with their plan. We can be sure, nevertheless, that it will be a good one when it is finally handed out to the order groups at the conference to which I am daily expecting to be summoned. A plan which, I should

27   and] added in 1st edn.

judge, relies on enticing the enemy forward, allowing him a good deal of ground on which to waste his substance, deceiving him as to our real allies by removing all weapons from those who rashly try to engage him now.

You needed quite a lot of old-fashioned liberal faith to believe in a democratic revival as the years went on. You needed, one of these journalists was saying in Paris, the Christmas of 1938, rather more than one glass of champagne to give the matter any kind of full-blooded attention. Not quite so much fun in Paris that year, or elsewhere, and in the intervals between the drinking perhaps an echo of the cannonade from south across the Spanish frontier where the guns of a holy and religious war were not necessarily silent for Christmas Day.

And in England? Well, we can all remember it, and a few newspapers, one or two old photos, a fragment of a diary, will serve to show our children all that we wish them to know of the manner in which we prepared for the revelation to come. And inside each heart, as the millions went homewards clutching unfamiliar gas-masks, fragmentary technique, was the thought that this might be no more than an evil dream, that at the last some lucky accident would deflect the blow. And yet if some man had arisen with proposals to arrest the tides or hold the sun in its course they would have called him mad.

Paris again, then, the day before the[28] war, Paris and the Gare de l'Est, watching the quiet lonely

28   the] added in 1st edn.

soldier standing apart from the rest, his dark, solemn, country face, eyes troubled, honest, reliable, obedient, unhappy. Would you not like to conceive of a world where they had left that boy on his farm, not taken him with his bundle of canvas-wrapped small kit to the Gare de l'Est, going up to the Line? I think we may take this conception to be common ground; and if we do not abolish war, let us at least outline a system which will leave the quiet and the peaceful and the home-loving to rest content.

Paris with the lights blue-dimmed—the evacuation commences? Yes, it commences notably. The far noise of shouting down the gusty spaces of the Champs Elysées is doubtless the enthusiasm of the populace manifesting itself for war. Well, it would be comforting to think so, but at all events the speculation is unnecessary. The noise you hear, stranger, is the shouting of American tourists who have been drinking handsomely and may now be said to possess the town.

There is perhaps something to be said for a nation that goes to war like this with tired resignation, saying—Let us make an end of this, let us have done with the farce of living that mobilizes us every few months away from our wives and children, and forces us to war every twenty years. There is something that is civilized, old-world, and courteous in this resigned abandonment. It is the tired, scholarly civilization to which the Chinese attained.

Expostulating with the drunken old anarchist, anxious to lean half-way out the carriage window, to be sick or to commit suicide, it is difficult to determine which.

Certainly, comrade, *c'est la guerre capitaliste,*[29] all right. *C'est la guerre,* anyway. Surely it is of many things the most ironic that you were just old enough to get into the last war and just young enough to get into this: and it is agreed among all of us—observe the whole carriage-full are in agreement—that it is also exceedingly ironic that you should have a great personal distaste for the causes and issues of both these wars.

And suppose again, comrade, that the capitalists do make the war, and that it becomes under their hands a different kind of war, that turns against them, and in which they themselves have to struggle to survive as human beings, let alone as capitalists? Have you considered the answer to that one, comrade, or deliberated on your actions in that event?

It may not be *la guerre capitaliste,* comrade, but it's a war all right.

---

29 The phrase occurs in an open letter from Lenin to B. Souvarin, published in *La Vérité* (No. 48), 27 Jan. 1918. Lenin is quoting from a speech of the leader of the French labour movement, Jules Guesde, to the General Congress of French socialist organizations, Paris, 1899.

Chapter Three

Throughout the bitter years before the war, each man followed whatever course seemed to him to be personally most satisfactory. We were young men in those days and asked questions of the world. Some of us, a little shaken by the bleak depression from which we had emerged, were pleased with work and money, though the money was as a rule insufficient and the value of the work illusory. Among my contemporaries in that time I can remember few whose work was satisfying to them, undertaken with belief—one or two scholars who went back into the past, a few scientists who asked no questions.

The happiest were those who were tough and naturally enlightened. Sometime in their youth they had knocked their heads against the system. After that they shook themselves and regarded the world distrustfully. You can't buck the system, they said— with truth. The old men—yes, and the young men, the yes-men, in the old men's places. With cynicism as a protecting shield, they watched with tolerant amusement the emotions of their fellows as the shadows so clearly indicated began to darken the sun.

The Great War—the first Great War—cut deep into a generation of men and tired out those who survived. In the bad years there was a wide gulf between the ignorance of our youth and the old men who had run the country for so long. The old men were tired men[30] and played for safety. The young men wanted action and belief and found neither. Between the two generations there grew up a genuine hatred, rare and peculiar to those times. We have been more fortunate in this war, and not so many men have been killed, and others of varying ages have learned wisdom, some even repentance, so that this cold, dividing hatred will probably not arise again; but it was a phenomenon, partly forgotten now, of the bitter years.

Throughout all this time we were searching feverishly for a belief that would persuade us to action. I know now that this search was a mistake. Educated and civilized men do not ask for faith and religion in their politics but go where the argument leads them. The demand for action that we made was a better and more natural symptom of our youth, and one that future legislators would do well to remember, since youth is a recurrent theme. No one ever took any action in the bitter years or even spoke out loud and bold. It was the era of prevarication, of the smooth parliamentary reply, the government commission, the committee of reference. So soft and well-cushioned was this system that protests fell blunted before they began their flight. In twenty years' time no one will believe that a desperate, frustrated

30   tired men] 1st edn. has 'tired old men'.

opposition existed. They will ask why we didn't get killed in Spain, assassinate Hitler, throw stones at our M.P.s. I don't know what answer we shall give except to plead natural cowardice and to say that the battle seemed lonely and hopeless and fought out in No-Man's-Land.

During most of these years, I was living in Oxford. Chance, rather than ability, set me among academic men whose minds had the perspective of more than one war and more than one generation. I was too young to appreciate then the quality of mind that comes from a disinterested search for truth, either scientific or historical. There were old men whom I met then whose life's work had gone into a Coptic dictionary or the editing of Anglo-Saxon fragments. My connection with them was amateurish and commercial. If I were to go back there now, I should feel a greater respect for them. At the time, I resented their aloof and suave disinterestedness, and failed to realize that they, more than most people, were building while the world burned. Few of them, unfortunately, had the complete unworldliness of a medieval grammarian which would have made their position more clear. They had succumbed in part to the cloistered and interior politics of a university world, and to brick houses[31] and rebellious children in North Oxford.

In the younger world of the university, which I belonged to and afterwards watched, there were

31 Mulgan's typescript originally included 'unloved wives' here; it has been heavily crossed out.

those queer contradictions of the English professional classes, social ease and sophistication and a general ignorance of the way men have to earn their living and fight and get knocked about and die. But since young men there had more time to argue than most, we covered a good deal of ground in our search for religion and belief.

Bad times are said to encourage religion. Certainly we sought for a religion or its substitute. Semi-political opiates like the Oxford Group were easy to avoid. They were harmless people who neither drank nor smoked, but ate too much and talked about themselves. To every generation its own faith-healer and it was our misfortune to provide Frank Buchman[32] with his hall of fame. There was often alleged to be some connection between Fascism and the Oxford Group, and there was, indeed, some kind of tenuous harmony uniting them. But British Fascism in its overt form was hardly palatable even for the well-to-do, with its raffish and imitative uniforms,[33] its combination of one-time prize-fighters and sexual guerrillas. A few earnest patriots like the late Lord Rothermere,[34] looking around for some form of social

---

32 A controversial American Lutheran minister, associated with the Oxford Group, and later with the foundation of the campaign for Moral Re-Armament.

33 uniforms] 1st edn. has 'uniform'.

34 Lord Rothermere (Harold Harmsworth) was an influential figure through the publication, in particular, of the *Daily Mail* and the *Daily Mirror*. For some time he actively supported Oswald Mosley, who belonged, in turn, to the Conservative and Labour parties, before founding the British Union of Fascists.

insurance, took up Mosley and found him too hot to handle.

British Fascism, when it comes, will be a polite and national affair in which the forms so dear to Englishmen are maintained and a lot of velvet covers the iron hand. Some people say that this is the state of affairs in which the English are living now; but personally I don't believe it. Parliaments live and die or become grotesque, as they did in the decade before the war; but in England the law-courts still function and judges criticize the executive, and while this happens there is no Fascism. And even those few in England who talked and thought Fascism, and may, for all I know, be thinking of it again, came out and fought in 1940 for something older and more primitive and, in this illogical way, contradicted themselves.

At all events, there was, in this earlier period, possibly a future, but certainly no appeal, to the young in Fascism. Only Marx in our time had church, gospel, and following.

Of many kinds of Communism that I have known since, this English version was the kindest and gentlest. I see that quite a lot of the comrades have reformed now. There has been a lot of repentance and acknowledgement of mistakes, and John Strachey[35] has discovered the principle of love. At that they were not the worst mistakes. It would be comforting[36] if, in this era

---

35 John Strachey, one time Labour M.P., was also a supporter of
    Mosley until the latter founded his Fascist Party. Strachey later
    established the Left Book Club.
36 comforting] 1st edn. has 'comfortless'.

of regeneration, a similar number of one-time Franco supporters, ambassadors who saw in Hitler a saviour from the Reds, and others who wouldn't offend Mussolini for fear of revolution, were coming forward now with the same noble sincerity of repentance. But perhaps these latter have been repenting, only more quietly. They know how disturbing it would be for the English to detect in their betters the horrifying evidence of fallibility.

The Marxism we studied had, like all religions, the defects of rigidity and dogma. (I was an amateur myself and made no sacrifices, not even of logic, but went along nevertheless. There wasn't anywhere else to go—except to the pictures and the public-houses, where, to be frank, I also spent a good deal of my time.) Some of the involutions of pre-war Communism seem fairly ridiculous now. I know that they always led the frequent protest meetings[37] on behalf of freedom of speech—surely not one of the tenets of the Master, and not a distinguishing mark of Communists when they come to power. I remember, though dimly, denunciations of the German Social Democrats in the happy year of 1933. I remember how they collected money from us to help French armament-workers on strike in the millennium year of 1936. Some of this might have prepared us for the great somersault of 1939, but it took a strong man to enjoy the smile on Stalin's face, pictured shaking hands with Ribbentrop, and featured in every paper in the world. Some of the young comrades called this the great betrayal; but we

37   meetings] 1st edn. has 'meeting'.

are realists now and know our way round in the field of power politics. I don't remember how the capitalist war of 1940 became the anti-Fascist war of 1941, but doubtless there is a good reason for it somewhere, worked out in pamphlet and dialectic. Most of us had got too busy and too uninterested by then to find out.

Even if the party was always right—an unlikely contingency, men and politics being what they are—their treatment of individuals was too coldly impersonal to offer much hope of a free and fair world. Communism in England was a parlour game as we played it. North and west in the mining and industrial districts I imagine it to have been a different kind of business, but even there, soft—by continental standards. When the debris of Europe is sorted out I hope to go back and find my friend Otto Strube, whom I last saw in Paris on the run, the end of August 1939. The party was going underground again, somewhat bewildered, a little contemptuous, but still taking orders. I would greatly like to know what happened to Otto, who had left his German wife, house, and family for the Party, who was still cheerful after concentration camps—Otto with his dark eyes and kindly, twisted smile, who had never grown too bitter to laugh at small jokes, and still enjoyed red wine, music, and sunlight, but was now a little puzzled in August 1939, and on the run again for a policy he couldn't understand. Otto was one of many, and it may be true that the individual has no place or importance in the fatal evolution of our times; but it is not hard to see the defects in a system which lays claim so coldly to individual men, and, being itself without humour or humanity, sets out to legislate for mankind.

And in an English world, there are other pictures that are less painful but not necessarily more hopeful. I had many friends who went into the Party like novices dedicated to a church. And afterwards trying to talk to them, feeling them withdrawn, very much alone, very proud and sure of themselves in the secret tenets of Marx, and finding myself again doubtful of a political system that embraces men so willing to escape from themselves, that offers this easy answer and refuge from decision.

Later on when we moved into Phase 2 of World War 2, I had some dealings with practising Communists. These were bearded gentlemen who killed their opponents or those that they thought might become their opponents. There was a good deal to be said against them and something to be said for them, and altogether they belong to a later and more serious passage of experience. Certainly they seemed to me, when I came among them, remote from the theories of those pre-war days.

But when they come to log up the regimental histories after the war, and particularly of the early days of the war before it became open and declared, I hope the comrades will write their histories too, for they also have their battle honours. They had the best battle honours before this formal war began, in many a dark street and prison and concentration camp, and

at Jarama, and Guadalajara,[38] Teruél, Brunete, and
the Ebro and Madrid, even at the end of[39] Madrid.
There were brave men before Agamemnon,[40] some of
whom knew the enemy and carried the fight to him. A
number of these campaigns were not very respectable,
and earned no medal ribbons, but will be remembered
nevertheless.

The search that we made for a political religion
and belief had no happy ending. While we searched
for something that could be both creative and stable,
war caught up on us again. We had never, in fact,
outgrown the shadow of that earlier war, which our
fathers had fought. It brooded over our thoughts and
emotions. Old wars take on dignity and grandeur. As
children we had heard men's stories, coming home,
had stood silent in parades of remembrance, knew
the names of old battles and heroes as part of our
lives. We felt the tragic waste and splendour of this
first Great War, and grew up in the waste land that it
produced.

If we had one resolve in common, it was that we
ourselves should not go the same way. We were not
trying to escape from fighting. The pacifism of this
period had in it no basis of physical fear. Most of us
were ready to fight. Later on we grew angry because
we were not allowed to fight. But we were determined

---

38 Jarama, and Guadalajara] typescript and 1st edn. both have
    'Jaramara, and Guadalamara'. The places named here are all
    significant sites from the Spanish Civil War.
39 of] added in 1st edn.
40 'vixere fortes ante Agamemnona / multi': Horace, *Odes*, IV. ix.
    25.

to avoid war on the insane and wasteful scale that our fathers had known, the kind of war that kills ten million people and leaves a worse world, that starts with rhetoric and morality, and ends with selfishness and recrimination.

We got our wish, in the sense that we got a different kind of war. But we might have known that no two wars are ever the same.

But in the period of which I am writing, we concentrated merely on tactics for the avoidance of war, and this fitted in well enough with the natural temper of the English, who are, at heart, deeply defensive. Up to the great depression, the idea of war was itself incredible. After that, when it looked possible again, the first move was to be pacific. We believed credulously in the efficacy of an international sit-down strike. This position was easily outflanked. It was turned and overrun in the early thirties. Our next defensive line involved fighting with a wide combination of allies, so many of them that the combination would never be attacked. This strategy was also pacific at heart. The implication was that nobody would ever need to fight. The diagrams in the staff-room with their interlocking fields of fire looked effective for a few months about the summer of 1935; but proved subject to increasing penetration in succeeding years—not to mention defection of the key fortresses and indeed of the commanders in our own sector. Until in the end, when the war really came home to us, in 1940, we came for a time to be merely defending ourselves, and that, while it lasted, was not unsatisfactory.

And after that, history, turning us over with the momentum of an ocean wave, threw us belatedly with Russians, Chinese, Americans, the disarmed millions of Europe, into a combined fight for survival, and that is where we had wanted to be.

It might have come sooner and in better and more hopeful circumstances, but it was, at heart, the situation that we had all wanted from the first. But, sadly enough, only the bitter logic of history and the aggression of other men's ideas had brought us to this desirable conclusion. We found nothing for ourselves. In the end, the war came to meet us and we fought it for our own defence. Nothing of the heart-ache and struggle for belief in the decade before the war bore any fruit. Only as we began to win the war did we realize this and know that we would have to begin to think positively again. We wasted a lot of time when we were young, and all you might say was that the years could be credited to experience.

Chapter Four

In the end the war came in, not with a bang but[41]a whimper. The sound of bombs falling on Warsaw did not carry across the wide plains of northern Europe. By the time it reached London the tumult was deformed into the soft reassurance of a Civil Service announcement. The same treatment had been applied to the bombs that fell on Shanghai and Chungking and Madrid and Barcelona, and by the same doctors, and it went on working well up to the end.

This was an odd period, the beginning of World War 2. It is not a time that the English talk about a great deal now. It's[42] passed now into the family annals, the volume that you keep in the cupboard and hope your executors will destroy. Everything that occurred in that long eight months was like an ugly caricature of what had gone before. It had elements of humour, but you needed to be an American to laugh at it.

Yet there was a quaint dignity about England in

---

41 but a whimper] 1st edn. has 'but with a whimper'. The alteration in the 1st edn. obscures Mulgan's allusion to the final line of T. S. Eliot's 'The Hollow Men'.

42 It's] 1st edn. has 'It has'.

those days, the air of an old gentleman taking out his uniform and saying, 'Gad, sir, we'll show these foreigners what sabre-fighting is.' Of course twenty years is too short an interval between wars. Twenty years means that everyone who knew what was what or, more important, who was who in the last one, moved easily back into the same offices and took over the files where they had left them. (The Germans unfortunately had a new set of files, not to say a new filing system.) Yet behind the quiet archaism of this approach to war lay something that hinted vaguely of better days—only you were not sure if the better days were in the past or were still to come. The sad friendliness of an old soldier's reunion lay over England then, and middle-aged gentlemen gave up their homes and wives, not always with regret, and settled down to uninterrupted evenings of port and bridge. Their manners were reassuring. They were perhaps a little inclined to cloud discussion of the present with reminiscences of the past; and, to this author's mind at least, they had[43] a genius for the inessential. But there was comfort in remembering that they had fought at Mons in 1914 and would fight there again, if they could find the way.

There was a sad little anecdote of this period that I like to remember, concerning a colonel with whom we once had some casual acquaintance. It seems[44] that his brigadier called on him, inopportunely, after a happy lunch that the colonel had passed rather too gaily with some old friends. This was in the early days before the

43 to this . . . they had] 1st edn. revises to 'they seemed to have'.
44 seems] 1st edn. has 'seemed'.

real war began, and you could still run your job on a city basis. He sat in his office looking at his brigadier, red-faced and alcoholically self-possessed. He was looking at the brigadier and listening to what he had to say but not really seeing him nor hearing him. He was recovering slowly from lunch and readjusting himself to the bleak monotony of the war, a war that was not yet like the last in comradeship and steadily increased excitement. This war was so far for him only odd bombs and questions of guards and billets and training manuals that had to be learnt again. The brigadier went on talking about some problem of accommodation and the guarding of vulnerable points, and in the end became dubious of this fixed, glassy-eyed attention, and said sharply, 'Well, what's the answer?' And the old colonel looked at him and concentrated carefully. 'There is no answer,' he said slowly, articulating with care, 'there is no answer.'

I like to remember this old gentleman—he was removed shortly afterwards from his post, not unnaturally—for drink had produced in him a rare descriptive honesty, and none of us in fact found easy answers at this time. I preserve, too, with pleasure the pregnant remark of a Cotswold farmer who summed up a bar-room discussion of man-power, reserved industries, and the like by saying firmly, 'Well, the last war they had, I kept rabbits.'

Not everything was pleasant or amusing. You could forget Poland; it was a long way away. But nearer home there were three hundred thousand Spaniards starving

in the sands at Pau.[45] (A construction engineer gave
us authentic news of them—'Tried 'em out on road-
making, old boy, no bloody good, half starved, sores
all over 'em.') It was still funny, but a little alarming,
to hear high-ranking officers discussing blandly the
advisability of declaring war on Russia—'One way to
get at the bloody Germans,[46] eh?' (In those days there
was a lot of talk about how to get to grips with the
Germans. Later on the Germans thoughtfully solved
the problem for the French and very nearly for the
English.)

There was a dreadful sobriety about the war also,
a sobriety that it never afterwards lost. It was never
really a war for martial music or patriotic slogans.
Later on we had another colonel who liked arranging
parades with music in the intervals of what might
be called ordinary soldiering. He never shared our
embarrassment on these occasions for he was a simple
man who liked his sentiment neat, and I think he finally
came to believe that 'There'll always be an England',
a song featured at that time by a comedienne, Gracie
Fields, had the status of a national anthem. Certainly
he used to look sharply at young officers who mixed it
in with their drinking songs.

Most people, however, continued to look on the
war as something demanding scrutiny and analysis.
Everyone examined it very carefully, holding the

45 Mulgan is presumably thinking of Camp Gurs, the internment and
    refugee camp in the south of France near Pau, set up after the fall of
    Catalonia to house those fleeing Spain after the Civil War.
46 Germans] 1st edn. has 'German'.

newspaper at arm's length, resisting every effort to enforce judgement. This was not the conventional way to treat a war and a smaller-sized war would probably have been adversely affected, but this war, as it turned out, was big enough to get along without much help from the sign-writers.

Most reassuring were the Englishmen themselves who were going to do the fighting. For there was a country going cheerfully off to war again with the same slogans, which didn't any longer apply, Bruce Bairnsfather and Bernard Partridge still drawing the same cartoons.[47] They were using the same weapons, except that some of the technique for using them had been forgotten, and only the men, a little damaged by twenty years of depression and uncertainty, were a constant factor on the credit side. Get you the sons your fathers got, and God will save the king.[48] Their fathers begot them when they could, and afterwards geography, the United States, the U.S.S.R., and the latent courage of the English were occupied for many years in saving the king.

The first men that I knew were steel workers and road workers and men from Cotswold farms. They were volunteers, spent one summer fortnight crawling along country hedges, fingering out-of-date equipment. They had a genial feeling at that time that one

47   Bairnsfather was a noted cartoonist of life in the trenches, having served at the Western Front in WW1; Partridge was the principal cartoonist for *Punch* from 1901 until his death in 1945.

48   The allusion is again to Housman's *A Shropshire Lad*. 'From Clee to heaven' (the first poem) concludes with the lines 'Get you the sons your fathers got, / And God will save the Queen'.

Englishman was worth any ten Germans. They had
no great faith in their officers and, as keen students of
the reminiscences that had been appearing in Sunday
newspapers, they had a profound contempt for generals
as a class. But they still had a good deal of belief in
themselves. They were drafted away that first November and, after a short interval in the fogs of Newbury
race-course, went overseas by packet-boat to France.
There they dug trenches, never to be manned, got
drunk on French wine, acted with splendid certitude
the part that they knew to be expected of Englishmen
abroad. One Englishman, they said, is ten Germans, is
ten Frenchmen too, they would add, but more quietly,
for politeness' sake. They crossed the frontier on May
10th, 1940, brown, shirt-sleeved, and singing. I didn't
see them but I have talked to those that did. They were
in reserve behind the Dyle; they were fighting ten miles
from Waterloo. They were bombed, got hungry, had
casualties, fell back through the lines that they had
spent a long, cold winter digging, as far as Bergue and
the Cassel hills. The ones that I am remembering now
were on the Cassel hills. They held their position there
for three days. No one that was with them there on
the last day had returned up to the time I was writing
this. They were surrounded, ran out of ammunition,
were overwhelmed, killed, or made prisoner. They
were beaten wherever they fought, not personally but
militarily, and always in retreat. They were defeated
by superior technique, better equipment, better
generalship. But I think if you meet the survivors now,
you will find them still confident, not at all malignant,

still happily convinced one Englishman is worth any ten Germans.

Other Englishmen in this time suffered none of these hardships but only the stagnation of war. Through all those first long winter months they stood around in cold and ice. It was a very cold winter. They guarded forgotten bomb dumps and railway bridges. I think half a million men spent their time like this, instead of training for war, protecting England against the depredations of a handful of Irish terrorists. Eager for action in all that time, they saw no evil, heard no evil, but spoke plenty. Having survived that period of unimaginable boredom, it's probable that they were prepared to survive more unpleasant things. I remember only that in mid-June 1940, when the bottom had fallen out of Europe and, it seemed, of the whole world as we knew it, somewhere in Southampton— the town full of disillusioned Englishmen from the bases in France, and bedraggled Frenchmen wanting to go home—somebody was calling for volunteers to go on some unspecified venture to the Continent, and all these soldiers wanted to go.

There was something breath-taking about the nonchalance of Englishmen at that time in 1940. The unhappy ones were amateur strategists, would-be intellectuals like this author,[49] who had foreseen ruin for so long and recognized it when it arrived. In military circles where I moved then, it was hard to raise any interest in the surrender of the French. Most simple Englishmen, God help them, were rather pleased

49   this author] 1st edn. has 'myself'.

to be alone—the full-back of freedom, somebody remarked—to engage in a war that they would ultimately win. And I remember how once, about that time, I was foolish enough to ask some soldiers what they thought we should do. 'Ah, shoot the generals and let's get on with the war,' one of them replied.

Later on, as the war went into its third, and its fourth, and its fifth year, the English came to think a little more coldly about the war and their place in the world, but this is the way they felt, for the most part, in 1940. It was a peculiarly maddening form of confidence, not least to their friends.

There is, nevertheless, a certain responsibility that devolves on the leaders of Englishmen. Someone will have to rationalize the situation before it is too late. There is not a great deal of time, in spite of the splendidly insane confidence that the English have in themselves. It is necessary to understand and clarify the organization, for the endurance that is called for now in the years in front of us is biological, and belongs to the community. It is no longer possible to survive on the splendour of individuals who are prepared to go out and get killed just for the idea of being Englishmen.

I had the good fortune in these years to serve with the British Army. We went to Ireland first and stayed there for what seemed like a long time, but is short now in the perspective of war. There we saw no action but only cold seas rolling on to cold northern coasts. We saw many other pleasant things and had good times. Most of the time we were training for a war that seemed to change every two or three months according to the

news from battle-fronts that were a long way away.
War became then something remote and theoretical.
It became more important to please visiting generals
than to be able to shoot straight or move quickly under
fire. But we had good times and a good sense of being
friendly together. The sense of friendliness that held
all the English together lasted well, though it never
regained the heightened quality of the summer of
1940. In the army we marched a lot and played a lot of
games. It was very pleasant, marching home at the end
of a long exercise in the field with everybody singing
and someone ahead in camp standing by with a hot
meal. These were the good times of war. They, too, get
heightened in quality under the stress of action, but real
war, the kind of war where people are getting killed,
has too many other problems to allow for much of this
happy Y.M.C.A. sense of fellowship. Still, it is nice to
remember, and not without value when we had it.

Some odd chance made me at one time adjutant of
a battalion. This was in the period when everyone was
trying to learn a new job, so I suppose one amateur
more or less did not matter, though I remember our
brigadier used to look at me oddly from time to time.
But in this capacity I found myself instructing officers
in the regiment's history. It had a good history whose
greatest moments came with Craufurd's Light Division
in the Peninsular War.[50] Some transient research done
in the intervals of compiling returns made me look

50 Brigadier-General Robert Craufurd commanded the recently-
    formed Light Division in a number of important battles in the war
    for the control of the Iberian Peninsula.

back, a little regretfully, to the time of the Iron Duke when England maintained an army that was small, competent, professional, tough.

In England, in modern times, the Air Force and the Navy have had a professionalism that is technical and circumscribed. They maintain a sense of exclusiveness in peacetime, and in war merely open their doors to favoured pupils without admitting the public. The British Army of peacetime is, on the other hand, only professional in the sense that a small number of officers and soldiers earn their living by belonging to it. Once war starts the British Army becomes the British nation. Its only exclusiveness is internal and centres round a system by which the professionals prevent the amateurs from taking charge. The Army that war evolves rather painfully over a series of disasters and the passage of time is something new, a creation of emergency. The Army belongs to the people in a way that the Navy or Air Force would never permit, though of course the people do not control the Army any more than they control the society they live in.

After the Great War, the British appear to have decided that their Army was inefficient, but that this was something like an act of God or a decision of nature that couldn't be altered. Montague's *Disenchantment*[51] and Lloyd George's memoirs[52] were

---

51 *Disenchantment* (Chatto and Windus, 1922) is a collection of essays about WW1, in which the author, C. E. Montague, served briefly on the Western Front before being transferred to Military Intelligence.

52 *War Memoirs of David Lloyd* George (Nicholson & Watson, 1933).

dissimilar but complementary reading on this subject. Soldiers are notoriously inarticulate so that their side of the case was likely to be less well expressed, but I don't think any of them could have dissuaded the public from the generally low view it held of the Great War's strategy, tactics, and management. There were too many casualties to explain away. When you have a lot of deaths to think about, the argument gets less than literary.

Why the British did nothing to alter all this, I don't know. They left themselves with little cause for complaint when the Second Great War started, since a country on the whole gets the army it deserves, and the British certainly deserved this one. England has no purely military tradition and soldiering has always failed to exist as a profession. Officers were not always hunting foxes but they never thought of treating war as a science. Sir John Moore[53] was unpopular because he took his work seriously. He probably talked about it in the mess. Marlborough and Wellington managed by a diversity of interests and aristocratic tastes to conceal their secret love for the art of war. When the English start to produce generals who think and work like professors of chemistry, they will be on the road to militarism.[54] They might begin, of course, by paying their Army so that officers can take up soldiering as a career instead of a part-time hobby and so that men

53 General, and commander of the British forces in Spain during the Peninsular War.
54 militarism] this word troubled those who prepared the text for publication, and some consideration was given to avoiding its negative connotations by substituting 'military efficiency'.

can go into the Army as to a job instead of as an escape from poverty and gaol.

The British Army had, nevertheless, one great gift to offer to[55] the nation. This was a system that had nothing to do with strategy and tactics but concerned itself with feeding and caring for a number of men and knowing how to carry out the detail of orders. The exponents of this system were the regular soldiers and N.C.O.s and they must have derived it in unbroken tradition from a long way back.

The innocent author of these reflections,[56] a keen pre-war reader of Tom Wintringham[57] and Trotsky, believed[58] at one time that all men were rational and if united in some common and fervent belief—like democracy or the rights of man—would provide all the necessary discipline themselves. This of course is untrue, as I had occasion to find out when I made an excursion into irregular warfare. The most fervent beliefs fail on a cold morning, or late at night in snow on the mountainside, and men who have been in the habit of providing their own discipline find themselves without it. It is possible that all men have within them the possibility of being rational, but that[59] for times of crisis and war the approved army system is more likely to be effective.

---

55 to] omitted in 1st edn.
56 The innocent . . . reflections] omitted from 1st edn.
57 Wintringham was a journalist, fiercely Socialist in his politics, but
     perhaps best known for his efforts to introduce guerrilla warfare
     training to the British Home Guard.
58 believed] 1st edn. has 'I innocently believed'.
59 that] omitted in 1st edn.

We have cause enough to be grateful to the old soldiers who held the Army together and taught us how to live and carry out orders. Most of them brought their knowledge from long years abroad in dust-dried barracks. There was some fragment of truth behind the Kipling legend. None of them had had much fun. They had led a life without the normal compensations that a man gets by making something or by working intelligently. Behind them lay the eternal gossip of military communities, the struggle to have children and homes,[60] a future of small pensions and menial jobs in civil life. But the bitterness and the system produced an austerity which is useful for war, and you thanked God when you met them—the straight-backed, humourless, reliable men, without imagination but also without temperament, who do what they say they will do and often get killed in the process.

When the war started, they co-opted a whole class of Englishmen on whom the British order now depends. The newcomers to the sergeants' mess were foremen from workshops, skilled mechanics, small farmers. Among men they are marked as technicians, able to produce their own kind of leadership. They have no great admiration for learning in the abstract, but appreciate knowledge that is immediate to their needs. Virtue lies in their essential independence and refusal to be patronized. They are men of a kind who place themselves in society more easily than other classes of men. Too many of us spend long, unhappy years in

60   homes] 1st edn. has 'home'.

pain and frustration, find out in the end the things we can and cannot do, the people we can impress or fail to move. A large part of the world fights a grim battle with poverty and physical want. But these others, the good craftsmen and foremen, are positive in their abilities. They know where they are going and usually get there.

Nearly all argument about the British Army fails to mention the soldiers who are running it and concentrates on the officers—who, it must be admitted, are fair game for comment.

Colonials are sensitive on this subject. I remember the time when our battalion, fresh to the desert, most of us novices to war, first came alongside the New Zealanders. These latter tried hard to hide the aversion that overcomes them whenever they meet an English officer, but you can always see how they feel. They hate the way British officers talk to their men—or did talk then—the accent of superiority and patronage. They dislike the way British[61] officers reckon—or did reckon then—that all their men are children from whom no mental effort can be expected, and so give detailed and petulant orders that no free-born man should have to suffer. They resent, too, the way British[62] officers have of maintaining one form of conversation and humour among themselves and a colder, stiffer form to other and lesser men.

Most of these things were superficial. I saw a change come over the Desert Army in a short period

61 British officers] 1st edn. has 'the British officers'.
62 British officers] 1st edn. has 'the British officers'.

of time. The battalions that came back from Tunis were welded into a new unity of a kind that I doubt the British Army had known before. Desert warfare had more to do with this change than any factor of morale or conscious desire to change. That curious unforgettable desert life threw men and officers together in small units; circumstances forced them into companionship. They lost nothing in discipline, gained greatly in mutual respect.

In my own observation, this only happened to men who had been in action together. It may for all I know have been merely a phenomenon of the Eighth Army and the desert; and the mammoth armies of the west may have continued with what soldiers call scornfully 'peacetime' conditions.

Something, at least, was wrong with the British Army, something that had to be altered before you could get the best kind of army—the army that is friendly and unified and at the same time effective. The young gentlemen of England do their best, of course. They always do their best, particularly in wartime. In peacetime, the young gentlemen can be average hell. They have few political vices. If they are Fascists, they are Fascists of a very unconscious and indolent type. I don't think the Führer would endure them for long in his party organization. They have a beautiful gift for depreciation, including depreciation of themselves, which would not endear them to the more serious members of the party. But their ignorance is wide and alarming and their acceptance of a social framework is as instinctive as the act of breathing.

In wartime they developed at once the standard virtues—courage, and character, and in some hesitating way a sort of kindliness. But all their education held them back from understanding other men; it needed battle and pain and sudden death to bridge the gap that they themselves created. Then, too, I think, you could charge against them that they reckoned to give orders without realizing the responsibility that devolves on those who give orders[63] in this world. In peacetime this may be all right—you have the money so you call the tune—though I doubt it's an ideal social system. In war, it no longer matters who gives the orders, nor in what accent, so long as the commands are effective. The best commands are those that carry conviction, and you need knowledge and ability for this.

This argument goes back a long way into English social life, for it is clear that the one good reason for the existence of a better-favoured class is that it should do the work that it has been chosen and educated to do. There is a lot to be said for having a small number of people about with nice accents and a sense of authority, but they need to realize why they are there. And that is why there still remains with me a vision of that sun-tried Desert Army, as a model of what men in the ugly business of fighting should attain to; and behind this belief lies a hope that this might remain as a lesson and an ideal.

Naturally, in the long years of occupational peace, man will forget the actual technique of fighting. If England reverts to the stupor of the last great peace,

63   without realizing . . . who give orders] omitted from 1st edn.

Army officers will slumber contentedly, satisfied that the vulgar amateurism of warfare is done with for a few years at least. They will tell stories of indiscipline and bad manners in the mess. They will look askance at young men who show any professional or technical interest in their work. I hope that occasionally, if such ill days occur again, there will come among them men who remember the Eighth Army of the desert and who will look at these others oddly, sitting over the port, as at men of a different world, remote from the language of war.

Meanwhile, of course, outside—in the barrack-rooms and the sergeants' mess—the men who have maintained the British Army up till this date will be playing 'brag', discussing women and beer, keeping watch and guard, holding themselves in readiness for the next time the big-shots want to put an army on the move.[64]

---

64 Mulgan's typescript included another paragraph here, deleted during his revision: 'These were all very general reflections, many of them purely theoretical. The war started slowly but it went on for a long time and in the end everyone that wanted had the opportunity to go and fight. It was very hard during all the period of training and talking and thinking about war to keep remembering that war was something that actually occurred. And in the end when one did come to real war, one found one's time taken up with absurd and almost personal problems. At least that was my experience. My own function in the army seemed to be, at one period, to have trouble with lieutenant-colonels'.

Chapter Five

The British Army attaches a lot of importance to the rank of lieutenant-colonel and naturally exercises a good deal of care in selecting men to hold the rank. This applies to regimental and active soldiering. On staff jobs and odd irregular establishments it's possible to be a lieutenant-colonel and not to be so carefully selected. A lot of my friends got to be lieutenant-colonels and they were no more than intelligent amateurs. One friend who was particularly intelligent got to be a brigadier. I was even a lieutenant-colonel myself eventually, not so much by intelligence, I guess, but by accident and decease. But the command of battalions and field regiments and the like went to steadier and more competent people.

This was as it should be. There isn't much responsibility on the lower levels in the Army. As a sergeant or a captain or a major, everything is very clearly laid down for you, the limits of decision are defined. But the commander of a battalion has about a thousand men under him to make or break. His power over them is more or less absolute. It rests with him whether the battalion works together and becomes a good fighting unit or whether it disintegrates. Of course, if he is a professional he will keep a steady eye on the brigadier next above him (some I knew kept both eyes firmly fixed in that direction); but the brigadier can't step in and take over the battalion. (Oddly enough brigadiers don't have much responsibility.[65] I expect major-generals and upwards have a good deal of say-so, but I was never close enough to observe them properly.)

The only trouble with the system is that, knowing the rank and command of a field unit to be important, the Army insists that all its regular officers should go through this step and bars them from higher staff promotion without it. This is an excellent idea, too, but you can see how, working steadily through the list, there must be names here and there that ought to be skipped. Of course, they're not skipped. Everyone agrees that old George, or whoever it is, must be given a break. Even when everybody knows that old George, though a shrewd judge of a polo pony, is barely of adult mentality in other respects, he has to be given this break. His colleagues and superiors who have known him for years (for the Army in peacetime is like nothing so much as a large club) have a touching belief that there may still be latent possibilities within old George. And, of course, if they didn't give him the break, he would have every cause to complain, and might even write a letter to the king.

The life of the ordinary serving amateur is

---

65 Oddly enough . . . responsibility] revised in 1st edn. to read: 'Oddly enough brigadiers in my experience don't seem to have so much responsibility'.

dominated in wartime by the lieutenant-colonels. Sometimes in moments of stress or resentment they seem to be like God. You will understand therefore that they need to be competent.

Regimental life is fine. Of many kinds of soldiering, I found it the best, the simplest, most straightforward, most satisfying. It has a pleasant corporate sense to it, rather like being at school again, with all the same adolescent emotions of playing for the side and being better than the next team. There is a lot of companion-ship and friendliness about it, and when the unit is working well everyone in it feels the same satisfaction of knowing they are good. And in the same way, if a battalion has a bad time and gets unhappy, everyone feels the disintegration. My first experience of active service was with a battalion that ran into trouble of this kind.

I joined a battalion as its second-in-command, at short notice, just two days before it left England. This was the period of the war when very few people had first-hand experience of fighting. The British Army was buying its experience at a high premium in the Western Desert, and that explains why an amateur like myself, with an ignorance of which I was very conscious, could be posted to such a position. Nothing that I remember of the battalion at that time is very happy. They had been hurried and muddled into mobilization for service abroad, made up with forced drafts, had changes of command and staff thrust on them at the last moment.

Time and subsequent history have brought me

gentler recollections of the lieutenant-colonel who commanded us.[66] I think he was as unhappy as they were in his command. He was young, not very intelligent, and obsessed with certain prejudices with which someone even more stupid than himself had once endowed him. He believed, for example, that all British soldiers were some kind of illiterate riff-raff whom only discipline and a barrack-square could control. He thought all his officers were in league against him in an effort to stop him commanding his battalion. When, later on, knowing him better, I tried diffidently to remonstrate against this attitude, he told me sadly that I was too young to understand these things or recognize the severe facts of army life. I think he found a kind of perverse glory in this situation. 'I've had some jobs handed me in my time,' he would say, 'but this takes it.' And again: 'You pay for promotion in this Army, you pay for it every time.' And he would shake his head at me, unsmiling, while we exchanged drinks over the saloon table. He was always more communicative when drinking. He liked drinking but did not drink very well. He talked more, but grew more sombre, if anything increasingly ugly in his views on those around him.[67]

---

66 Identified in *Long Journey to the Border* (p. 239) as Jock McAlester.

67 The whole of this paragraph was removed from the 1st edn. In its place, the following sentences appeared: 'The lieutenant-colonel who commanded us was as upset by this haste as the men and, like them, unhappy in the command. He had the characteristic views of the regular army officer on discipline and the British soldier. These were to my mind prejudices, and so it was not unnatural that I

I don't think there was anything wrong with the battalion, except that it was unhappy and not yet welded together. I knew very little about soldiering, but something about men in different parts of the world. This battalion was like any other British battalion, its men as willing to fight as any sensible men are who know that they must leave their homes and undergo the unpleasantness of war. None of the officers ever criticized this lieutenant-colonel[68] to me. I think they probably had criticisms to make but observed that curious loyalty which the British Army numbers among its traditions. I don't think their commander understood anything of this. He moved in lonely arrogance, a leader confronting destiny with indifferent material.[69]

The troopship in which we journeyed to war seemed to move very slowly. We went southwards, doing our fifteen knots, hour after hour. We went down through the Atlantic and under the Southern Cross, paused for three days in South Africa to drink Cape brandy, turned north into heat that was wet and intolerable. While we were still at sea the Germans took Tobruk and drove into Egypt. We landed in Egypt and after a brief fortnight went up into the desert. It was midsummer and very hot. Dead still lay unburied after the fighting on Ruweisat ridge and on Miterya, and flies were thick, hairy, and clinging. It

---

should differ from him a good deal about the battalion, though our differences never went beyond occasional arguments'.

68   this lieutenant-colonel] 1st edn. substitutes 'the command'.

69   I don't think . . . indifferent material] omitted from 1st edn.

was a period of low morale[70] in the British Army and the divisions we met on the Alamein line were not encouraging. They were still undefeated but bitter and uncomprehending and contemptuous of their generals. We extended the line southwards towards the Qattara Depression and dug trenches into the desert flint.

Nothing happened for about ten days except for shelling by night, none of which touched us, and odd planes by day. We began to get dysentery and desert sores which were the hall-mark of that campaign. The battalion took heart from having work to do at last. The first edge of active service is stimulating so that for a time one's senses and apprehension are sharpened and small personal troubles diminished. We all knew that there would be a long period of time before we could ever have any true knowledge of desert fighting, but the strange fascination of that waste land began to take hold of us.

The Germans attacked again at the end of August. It was the last attack that they made in the desert and, though we did not know it then, this was the end of the desert offensive that had begun long years before and run over Europe and Africa and ended that autumn at Stalingrad and Alamein. This last attack was neither very elaborate nor very determined but had within it the hopeful intention of ending in Cairo.

The main advance was south of us, probing in through the no-man's-land by Himeimat, feeling for the back of the Alamein line. The night that it

70   period of low morale] typescript has 'low period of morale'.

started we were moving into a new forward position and caught the weight of a barrage that was intended to cover the flank of the attack. The night was ugly with confused menace, nobody knowing what was happening. The firing went on all night but we had no casualties. War is reassuring like that, when all you have to do is to[71] stay in a trench. The sun came up with red regularity and brought its accompanying flies. Anything, I found out afterwards, in war is bearable[72] so long as some routine and familiarity can be brought into it.

We spent four days like that peacefully enough and then were ordered out with the rest of the brigade for a night-attack. By this time the Germans had gone some miles into the south and were looking for somewhere to attack, but appear to have found more troops or a better general than they expected and were not doing very much attacking. The plan was now to worry them by moving by night across the line that they were using for their supplies.

From Alam Nyal, the ground rolled in ridges down to the edge of the Qattara Depression, broken by escarpments and the fantastic little peak of Himeimat. None of these features seemed very pronounced or important at first until one came to fight or take cover in them and then each ridge or spotted height upon the map began to have a considerable value of its own. Only a few miles south of Alam Nyal, the

71　to] omitted in 1st edn.
72　Anything, I found out afterwards, in war is bearable] 1st edn. has 'Anything in war, I found out afterwards, is bearable'.

southern corner of our line, was the Munassib, a canyon of soft sand running east and west, its hills blown into odd shapes by the wind, a good safe hidden route for transport. This was the main line of the German advance. The plan was for the brigade to move out towards it, get near enough and dig in, and get artillery shooting into it.

Nobody in the battalion felt very comfortable about this attack. We were all of us too new to desert fighting to have any confidence or exact knowledge as to what we should do, and everything was very hurried. Our commander had always despised the detailed planning and imagination which are needed for efficiency in war. He hated staff officers and their necessary methods. I remember one evening on board, when he had been unfavourably compared with some of his colleagues over some question of military theory, his calling me into his cabin on my way to bed and inviting me to drink to the confusion of all military theorists. 'I can't argue with them,' he said. 'They can keep all their staff college paper. But I'll be interested to see them there when the shells start falling.' He was, I remember, very excited over this. 'By God, yes,' he said, 'when the mortars come down—whee-ee-e' and he made a sweeping gesture with his hand that cracked the glass on the cabin basin. So we shook hands then on the idea of being men of action. 'You'll see only fighting if you come with me,' he said, 'just ordinary fighting, by God, no three page orders.' So we shook hands on that, two tough fellows that were just going out to fight and not worry about any military theory.[73]

Everything that happened[74] the night of this attack was not any person's fault but a combination of them and mostly the combined total of our general inexperience.[75] Afterwards, when we learned a little more, I could understand how, to succeed in something so complex as a brigade night-attack, each person must have projected[76] himself into the plan and imagined[77] each contingency, and then laid[78] down a series of definite orders for his own part in it. And, having done that, he must have confidence in the unit with which he was[79] moving and know that there would[80] be no deviation from the plan.

It was still light when the brigade formed up on the face of the Alam Nyal ridge, too light, and shells began falling in the marked gaps of the minefields below and went on falling there through the night. After a lot of confusion, and some genial swearing from a New Zealand brigadier, everybody[81] got into

---

73　Our commander ... military theory] all omitted from 1st edn.
　　which substitutes: 'There was little time for preparation and our
　　commander had always believed that fighting spirit could redeem
　　any lack of minute planning'.

74　Everything that happened] 1st edn. revises to 'What happened'.

75　but a combination ... general inexperience] 1st edn. revises to 'but
　　was mostly due to the combination of our general inexperience'.

76　have projected] 1st edn. revises to 'project'

77　imagined] 1st edn. revises to 'imagine'.

78　laid] 1st edn. revises to 'lay'.

79　was] 1st edn. revises to 'is'.

80　would] 1st edn. revises to 'will'.

81　everybody] 1st edn. revises to 'everyone'.

place and began to move off. I was not going with
them but had orders to stand by for the morning
and find them in their new position. The battalion
went past very quietly three abreast, and after them
the second battalion of the brigade, and then a lot
of transport, carriers, and anti-tank guns. The dust
swirled up in the track as they went past and then they
were down the hill, through the mine-field and the
sound was shut away from us and the desert seemed
empty and still again. Somewhere up to the north a
series of white flares went up and floated in the air
for a while and after that the whole night was dark.
Odd shells went on falling south of us in the direction
of the brigade's attack but they sounded remote and
harmless. It is never easy to feel personally the fire
that is falling on other men. The moon, four days past
full, came up and lighted us back to our bivouac area.
We rolled up in blankets and slept there, waiting for
news of the battalion.

News came early in the morning and all of it
was bad. The brigade had gone forward, packed in
close formation, its transport clanking noisily with
it, had advanced too far on to the forward slopes of
the Munassib Depression, into a hollow where enemy
positions almost enclosed it from three sides. Halted
there, it had been fired into cheerfully by Germans and
Italians who lit the valley up, at first with flares and
then with the flames of burning vehicles. The brigade
had[82] stayed there long enough to collect a bitter quota
of casualties and then had fallen back, disorganized,

82   had] added in 1st edn.

and was now waiting on the ridge just forward of the minefield. We heard all this in the morning as a new sun, still red, was coming up, and then went forward to find the battalion for ourselves.

Nobody knew very accurately where we should go, but we went down the track through the minefield and stopped before we came over the open ridge to ask an anti-tank gunner. 'I wouldn't know,' he said, 'all I know is I fire on everything comes up the track and there hasn't been anything come up yet.' He was a New Zealander, and grinned at us: 'I wouldn't go too far out in front,' he said, 'Old Jack's out there.' That meant Rommel. They always called him Ted or Jack, as one way of showing that they didn't worry very much about him.

We went over the ridge and through the second minefield. There was another ridge out in front of us about a thousand yards away, and in the hollow between there were a few trucks and odd people scattered about. Away to the west was a high point of ground that we knew belonged to the Italians. There was a good deal of movement around it, of a kind that was hard to distinguish, small black specks of men scrambling and standing about on it.

There was a dead man lying in the entrance to the gap and we drove round him. He had the battalion colours showing on his helmet, but I couldn't see his face nor who he was. He lay very naturally on his back, with his knees bent up as if he might be resting, his equipment neat and untouched and no wound showing, but with that curious limpness that the dead always have. Odd shells were falling on the flat, out in front of us, and one or two started to arrive on the ridge behind us. We drove a little faster but there was no great satisfaction in speed; the flat of the valley seemed very naked and open.

The brigade-major was in charge of what was left of the brigade. He was an Irishman and seemed to be quite happy, giving orders to six tanks that were cruising round asking for a chance to come home and get out of this stupid and open place. After that he was sitting on top of a truck telling an artillery officer what he wanted. This brigade-major was the only coherent man we met all that day. I suppose one is enough in any battle, especially a battle that is as catastrophic as this one seemed to be. He was killed two months afterwards at Alamein, but this day he was very alive and cheerful and confident and encouraging to meet. The brigadier and two of the three colonels from the brigade had been wounded. He told us where to find our own battalion and commander.

This didn't take long. As we drove over the foolish little patch of sand where the remains of the brigade had collected itself, odd shells puffed up the sand. Every hill and ridge that the enemy held seemed to look down into this hollow, and behind us, going back to the safe and friendly line of Alam Nyal, were the tracks through the minefields, painfully clear and ranged upon accurately. While the sun was rising the enemy looking eastwards were blinded, but now it was climbing quickly and the general effect was undesirable. Six Stuka bombers—this was in a late, archaic[83] period of the war when Germans still had aeroplanes—flew over us, their black and yellow crosses glinting in the sun, very low, and dropped their bombs on the gun positions behind Alam Nyal and then flew back over us disdainfully.

There wasn't very much of the battalion to find. There were about a hundred of them left. Others drifted in during the next day or two, men who had been slightly wounded or got lost, but at the moment there were about a hundred staying out in front there. They were dug in or scraped into the ground in a half-circle looking west and south. The remains of the second battalion took on from the left. We went round them, stopping to drop off some of the small stock of water we had brought with us, and gathered the story of the night's disaster as we went. It began to occur to us that the day would be a long one and would seem longer still to those who had survived a night of the same kind of thing.

Demoralization is an ugly word. Nobody in fact attacked the battalion all that day. The enemy was pulling back fast, out-generalled, I guess, and a little frightened, but none of this was apparent to the men crouching there who had seen all their friends killed in a gesture of an attack, and now wanted just to get away back somewhere, where the positions they held and the trenches they manned would make even limited sense.

We found the doctor in against the small slope of a hill. He had lost his own truck and all his equipment

83   late, archaic] omitted from 1st edn.

and was working with some New Zealanders. His glasses had come off in the night, leaving him short-sighted, and the mine that had blown up his truck had partially deafened him. He was a friendly little man, a Polish Jew from Dublin, the kind of man that is conscientious and likeable and that you feel needs protection. He was getting very little now. Casualties were coming in from the shelling and they still had men about from the night before that they had been unable to get away. He looked like a man who would soon be very tired. Oddly enough his first impulse was to apologize to us for having lost his truck and ask for permission to stay with the New Zealanders and help there. This didn't strike us at the time as an occasion for technical arguments. We left him some water and tried to say something encouraging to him, but he couldn't hear, so I smiled at him and patted him on the back and left him. I hope he survived this war (he saw more of it than most people), for he was one of the kind and deserving that we shall need eventually.

A little farther on we found the colonel. He was sitting in a trench by himself. I expect he felt more or less like hell. A lot of work goes into the making of a battalion, even a bad or an unhappy one. A part of everybody that has belonged to it goes into it. It is something that lives and has an entity and spirit of its own, so that when you see a battalion that you command broken as this one was, you feel the hurt of a living organism, quite apart from all personal feelings that you may have for friends and individuals that have been lost.

We went back and forwards and twice through the minefield gap to the shelter of Alam Nyal to bring more water and some food down. It turned out to be a long day, as we had expected. In the desert, in summer-time, a mirage from the heat and glimmer of the sun clouded all visibility from midday onwards and was never so blessedly welcome as on that day. But towards evening, as always, the sun declining westwards brought the desert again into sharp relief, and those who were still there felt again the nakedness of being silhouetted against an enemy target. I remember, in the late afternoon, the bitter swearing of a man we picked out of a trench, who had survived what he reckoned to be enough, and had been hit finally, his shoulder almost severed, by an air-burst shell as he lay in the shallow comfort of his slit trench.

As it grew dark the brigade withdrew, men singly stealing through the minefield gaps, and trucks following them at long intervals. They went back into the bivouac area within the New Zealand lines to gather themselves together again. The whole battalion had to be made over again. A few days later the colonel who had commanded us left. I don't know why, or who decided he should go, or even where he went. I never saw him again. We never talked about him. I should reckon him to have been unlucky not only in his command but in his time. I expect he had better and luckier times later in the war which, after all, went on long enough to let anyone who cared to hazard it lose and re-establish a reputation two or three times.

If he should[84] read this now, he would not recognize it as referring to himself because I know it is quite different from the picture that he had of himself, and, indeed, it may well not be the true picture that I have written down here, but only as it seemed to us at the time.

Those of us who were left behind began to try and rebuild the battalion. You will appreciate that there was no great feeling of confidence or eagerness for war in the battalion at that time. Men are often marked by their first experiences[85] in war and this had been a bad one. Only the good people who had been through it grew out of it individually. The others had to rely on the slow tempo of allied victory that began at that time. They had lost confidence in their leaders, but did not need much intelligence to appreciate the flow of armaments and aeroplanes that they began to see around them. They reacted slowly and dubiously, like men who have been fooled twice and do not want to go down the same road again.

We had a good colonel[86] after that. He was so good that all of us count it an honour now when he remembers us as friends. He worked very hard and put heart back into the battalion and into all of us. We all felt so bitterly about the misfortune and ill luck that we had had, that we were prepared to work

84 should] added in 1st edn.
85 experiences] 1st edn. reads 'experience'.
86 a good colonel] 1st edn. substitutes 'another colonel'. O'Sullivan identifies him as Colonel Lambert; see *Long Journey to the Border* (p. 248).

with him always and do everything that he wanted. He took us into the battle of Alamein and made it by comparison a picnic. I think generals were treating us lightly as dubious material. I know that after we had followed up a diversionary attack in the south and watched the tanks that should have broken through strand themselves on a minefield, we were left not unhappily occupied on a plain underneath Himeimat, in a position that could have been as suicidal as our first experience of desert attack. It was overlooked in the same way and equally wasteful of casualties, but there were so many guns behind us anxious to fire at the first shy Italian who left his trenches, and so much more was happening to the north of us, that we felt almost idyllically safe. In the last nights of that ten days' battle, we could watch the barrage creeping forward in a long roll of thunder to Kidney Hill and know that at least the enemy as well as ourselves would be preoccupied.

We could claim small part in this victory, but it was something to have been there and to drive forward afterwards through trench systems and minefields that had dominated our lives, and count the thousands of thirsty Italians streaming home. The feeling of victory around us was all that we needed. The battalion had been through a bad time and had come to rely on itself. Now this reliance and confidence could extend itself and become general.

The colonel who had done most of this for us left soon afterwards. He was, of course, too good to stay. The very good and the very bad move around quickly in wartime. He left us for promotion and we stood by with some apprehension for the next.[87]

I don't know who was picking colonels for us at that time; if perhaps some sardonic spirit back at headquarters was looking around to see how much the battalion would take before it mutinied; or, more probably, since we were not fighting then but resting and refitting, someone reckoned that it didn't matter, that this was a good time to work over some dubious name on the list.[88] The battalion was very happy at this time,[89] but whoever knew them or remembered their recent history would have known that this new confidence was delicately balanced against an old despair. They would have known, too, that as a battalion they were suspicious of colonels.

The new arrival was one of the most charming individuals that I met in army life.[90] He was middle-aged with a quiet and friendly voice, he had something of a reputation as a cricketer, you could see at once that he wanted to be on good terms with everyone, you might almost have said that he wanted to please. It only took about a fortnight for it to become apparent that he was, roughly speaking, ga-ga.

I don't know how this new colonel of ours had passed his twenty years' service, but I can guess. Scraps of background were filled in for me during our brief acquaintance. A long spell abroad, garrison duty

---

87 He left us . . . for the next] sentence omitted from 1st edn.
88 I don't know . . . on the list] sentence omitted from 1st edn.
89 at this time] 1st edn. has 'during this period'.
90 Identified in *Long Journey to the Border* (p. 249) as S. F. Saville.

in India, no fighting, a longer spell as adjutant of the regimental depot; in wartime, odd jobs of staff and liaison duty, never any fighting, nor any acquaintance with war. In all this time his mind—not at any time, I suspect, very acute—had atrophied, so that his conversation was now no more than fragments of personal reminiscence. He had difficulty in following any connected discussion. I used to watch him with pencil and paper trying to work out some difficult military problem like the orders for a battalion church parade and, after about quarter of an hour of scribbling and erasion, giving it up and handing over the problem to the adjutant and going out to smoke cigars in the sun. But a nice man, a charming, friendly person—I felt towards him as to a child, that I would like to protect him and look after him. I could never feel any animosity towards him or want to harm him.

I don't know what prompted me, a month later, to take the action I did. A sense of belated responsibility, perhaps, to the battalion and to the general prosecution of the war. We all grow up eventually. Also a mild feeling of anger and frustration against a system that would allow incompetence, like any other peacetime luxury, to flourish in war.

There isn't any recognized procedure in the Army for protesting against the incompetence of one's seniors, or if there is I, at least, never found it in King's Regulations, and so was forced to improvise. I asked for an interview with this colonel and told him briefly, I think politely, that I thought him incompetent—I would have preferred to use the word incapable, but it carries the wrong connotations. [91]

This needed a considerable effort. Now that I have left soldiering,[92] I can't so easily recapture the atmosphere of army life, where[93] the personality and opinions of senior officers are sacred. I know that everything I had been taught in three years of war about army tradition fought against what I was doing. No military discipline will survive the anarchy of subordinates questioning the next man above them. We were even trained, probably rightly, to hold back from any general discussion in the mess which might prove a senior officer wrong. I have watched well-disciplined dons of the older universities writhe in an agony of silence while foolish and illiterate old men supported some popular fallacy. There are no medals awarded for this kind of spiritual merit, but it ought to be recognized by some special plaque to commemorate a strong and enduring sacrifice.

We faced each other across the table while I explained, in words carefully chosen after many hours of thought, the difficult[94] proposition that I wanted him to embrace. I don't know what I expected, but

91 It only took about a fortnight . . . carries the wrong connotations] preceding paragraphs omitted from 1st edn. which substitutes: 'In spite of this it was soon apparent to me that we differed completely as to the handling of the battalion. Eventually, I asked for a formal interview and expressed this disagreement'.

92 soldiering] 1st edn. has 'regimental soldiering'.

93 atmosphere of army life, where] 1st edn. has 'atmosphere in which'.

94 difficult] omitted in 1st edn.

probably that I should be put under arrest. In fact, he looked at me wryly without speaking for a time and I had the sad conviction that in one way or another all his life men above him had been telling him of his incompetence. The experience of someone junior doing this was perhaps novel, as he began by remarking. 'This,' he said gently, 'is something a little foreign to my experience. I'd no idea,' he went on, still gently with a sort of soft and foolish melancholy that I found attractive, 'that things were as bad as all that. Of course I know very little about what's going on. You must help me more. Come in at any time.'[95] And[96] he shook me warmly by the hand and I found myself leaving the tent feeling like a man who has nerved himself to jump from a great height and finds himself arrested in mid-air by bales of cushions.

In later times, when I grew more cynical, I sometimes wondered whether this had not been a shrewd and disarming technique. At least I remember finding it very difficult to proceed. Only the pressure and proximity of war made me realize that no one could continue in this[97] situation. The battalion would be going into action again and someone would have to command it.[98] I reformulated my statement in writing, in grave Johnsonian English, the kind of balanced periods that happily still survive in King's Regulations, and asked for it to be forwarded to

95 In fact, he looked at me . . . at any time] all omitted in 1st edn.
96 And] 1st edn. substitutes 'Instead'.
97 this] 1st edn. substitutes 'my'.
98 The battalion . . . command it] sentence replaced with 'It was a difference in principle and seemed to me important'.

higher authority. Higher authority has a quick way of dealing with such subversive[99] documents. My resignation from the battalion was accepted. The gesture—it was little more—had not been altogether wasted. After a decent interval the colonel left also, and before the battalion went into action again.[100] This was one of the battalions that made history at Kohima and won for itself a name that will long be remembered among professional fighting men.[101] The brief flicker of a personal mutiny which I conducted would be remembered only as a friendly reminiscence among those who survived fifteen months of fighting in Burma, and no one asks for more than that[102] in wartime—that he should be kindly remembered by those with whom he served. Even this gentle little colonel probably thinks less harshly of me now. The army looked after him, as is the custom, and I am sure he is happy somewhere, occupying some staff position with dignity if not with devastating efficiency.[103]

Nevertheless, I knew from this time onwards[104] that the first essential of command in wartime[105] is competence. Personal charm, or savage discipline, or individual bravery are good things in their place and

---

99 subversive] omitted in 1st edn.
100 The gesture . . . action again] sentence omitted in 1st edn.
101 fighting men] 1st edn. adds 'The colonel had left before this campaign'.
102 that] 1st edn. reads 'this'.
103 Even this . . . devastating efficiency] omitted in 1st edn.
104 Nevertheless . . . onwards] 1st edn. reads 'By this time I had seen enough of war to know'.
105 in wartime] omitted in 1st edn.

at the right time; but men, I knew now, would forgive any vices in a commander so long as he was capable. I began to suspect also that bravery itself in war was a matter of competence and organization.

Chapter Six

In the days when we were talking and thinking about war before experiencing it, everyone tried to imagine the real state of warfare. Enlightened commanders brought in live ammunition and explosives to stimulate training. Battle-schools were all the rage. I was personally a great success at battle-schools. No one could plunge more courageously through a storm of bullets and exploding '808' than myself, knowing that the whole affair was effectively controlled by marksmen who knew their business.

We had two theories about war and the individual then. One was that you needed to have some inner faith to sustain morale—that is to say, you would fight very passionately, and perhaps die, for democracy or the Four Freedoms.[106] The other, or battle-school theory, was that war is only noise and confusion, something, in fact, that you can get used to. Neither of these two theories turned out to be correct.

---

106 The reference is to an address to Congress by Franklin Roosevelt, 6 June 1941. To the traditional Constitutional freedoms of speech and religion, Roosevelt added freedom from want, and freedom from fear.

How to get Faith, or the Will to Win, was a question that worried us greatly in the early days. It grew by reaction from the claims that Fascism was making for itself. In the long, bad years, democracy was said to be on the defensive. In fact, democracy was[107] about as much on the defensive as a hypnotized rabbit. Fascism was said to be the new faith, the new order, and Nazi fanatics took rank with the first Mohammedans. All sane men knew that Fascism was evil—some men were prepared to make a pact with Fascism for reasons of private interest but even they, I think, knew they were trafficking with the devil. Those men who wanted to fight Fascism looked round for an idea to fight it with. (I imagine they thought they had better have an idea since anyone who, more straightforwardly, took a gun was immediately disarmed by his fellows and told not to disturb the peace.) Meantime Fascism went on winning.

Opposition to the new faith and order came from the Left and so did the ideas to fight with. But the Left was deeply imbued with a pessimism of its own. I don't know from what this sprang (Lenin never suffered from it), but all the Left of Europe in the pre-war years was bitterly prophetic of defeat. The doctrine of each man was to die fighting, never to win. At best some distant generation might draw benefit from Russia, but for ourselves the martyr's crown. Few people on the Left admitted this aloud, but you could see it in their eyes, in the dogged, cynical way of speech, in the timorous plan of campaign.

107 said to be . . . democracy was] omitted from 1st edn.

I know now that many of us unconsciously shared this pessimism as the long chain of Fascist victory unwound, and in 1940 were prepared to see England go the way of France and ourselves fighting still more hopeless battles in the streets.

In the end Fascism, the idea, broke on nothing except old-fashioned nationalism, first in England, then in Russia. You never found Churchill worrying about one ideology or another in June 1940, only about Germans and English. Myself, I drew comfort from our quartermaster, who had seen the last war through and twenty-five years' service, and in all his life had never considered any kind of politics nor any kind of defeat. At the time, I reckoned he was crazy but I was tired of ideas by then. I thought then that if I had to stay with anyone, this was the kind of man to stay with.

But after 1940, while we went on training and never fighting, the mood passed. Attack seemed a long way off but we knew then that eventually we would go over to the offensive, and the nagging search for a faith returned. It seemed that old-fashioned patriotism could save a country but not take it to the attack, that sooner or later men would be asked to die on the beaches of Europe and that for this they would need something more than a sturdy English irritation against foreign invaders. You could see this unquiet search for an idea reflected at the time in the demand for declared war aims, Atlantic Charters,[108]

108 Document negotiated and agreed to by Churchill and Roosevelt in August 1941 setting out eight key goals for a post-war world.

and Four Freedoms. Myself, I regret to say, I worried a good deal over this—unlike our quartermaster who was still doing his original, competent job—until in the end I came to see that none of this was affecting the English, that the idea, when we found it, might be a good weapon of war against the enemy, but was not necessary to ourselves at all.

Common men no longer start wars: they take part in them[109] when someone else has started them. War nowadays is a major accident and calamity, it is a storm that is seen a long way off. First of all the scientists chart it; they send out terse messages to say that it is coming, but few people listen to them, only other scientists understand them. Old men read the meteors, but they have prophesied war so often that they may be wrong this time. A little later there are dark clouds a long way off on the edge of the sea and streaks of windy sky. Look-outs, far-sighted men, and travellers flying home before the gale cry aloud that this is a great storm, such a storm as wrecked the island twenty years before. Many people are alarmed at this; they look to their basements and flood-proof shelters, but there are still left many others who say this storm will not come to us, it will go by on the east or the west as it did last year and the year before. In the end, just before nightfall, there is no doubt that the storm will come. The whole sky is dark overhead and the sea is stirring uneasily and the first heavy drops of rain are falling. At this point the old man, the chief of the village, makes an announcement. It is

109 them] added in 1st edn.

not very easy to hear him above the rising wind. He says that there is a great storm coming, of a kind and severity that visited the island twenty years ago, that they will take the same measures which answered so well in the past, and that in the end it will go from them. Soon after that there is darkness and the storm is upon them, and they work through the night fighting the storm together.

This is the way war comes now, at least to a country like England where men are not politicians. The English work along and take what comes. Sometimes it is all right, it is a good summer or a prize in the football pools; more often it is something less palatable. It is a depression or a bad harvest and in the end, once every generation or slightly less, it's[110] a war.

But there is a very definite understanding amongst the English that, whoever starts the war, everyone takes part in it. They may not like the war very much and be sceptical of its reasons and benefits, but they go into it together and stay together until it is finished and only then do they disinterest themselves. The English are a family and at every crisis in their family life, like a wedding or a funeral or an eviction, they act as one.

This is one reason why it is difficult to take the English into a war except on some good, moral and inescapable pretext. The morality may not stand up so well in history, but they must be able to believe it at the time, or feel themselves attacked, before they will commit themselves to war.

110 it's] 1st edn. has 'it is'.

There is probably a lot to be said for having an army whose individuals have a private and passionate feeling about the war and who, because of this, do not mind at all what happens to themselves personally. But armies of this kind are more rare than is commonly believed. They flare up in some cause, usually lost, and die, and soldiering takes on again the cool precision of the Illyrian legions. This kind of army is more often found in defence than in attack. It fights on its home ground when the issues are desperate, as[111] before Madrid in 1936. There would have been an army, several armies of this kind, in England in 1940 if the Germans had arrived. I believe there was an army of this kind in Russia for the first bitter winter of their war and probably for as long as the Germans stayed in Russia. This kind of army is clearly very difficult to deal with and professional soldiers are apt to regard the whole proceeding as unmilitary, which indeed it is.

There have been religions in history which produced armies of the same kind and took the offensive in successful crusades. Most of them worked by promising immortality, an excellent donative so long as you believe in it. Few of them lasted for long. Old soldiers get together round the fire and grow sceptical.

Successful armies have sometimes nourished a similar faith in their invincibility; they have made us feel that they must win because their soldiers had this same personal disregard for everything except victory. This view is better in propaganda than in

111 as] typescript has 'like'.

analysis. These are the armies that go places because they know they are winning. They develop a splendid disregard not for their own personal safety but for the opposition. The French who fought at Valmy were an army of the first, bitter, desperate kind, fighting for their revolution in their own country. Afterwards, when they went over Europe under Napoleon, they had developed into that other kind of army that knew it was good.

The Germans in France in 1940 flourished the same kind of illusion as one of their weapons. They had something at that time, they also had all the guns and the tanks and twice the number of men. It is possible to take one or two risks on a proposition of that kind.

It seemed to me finally, on further analysis, that two different sets of belief were needed for the business of war. One was basic and general and was required to sustain men and women through the long years and the[112] lonely winters. This, with the English, was a deep and lasting faith in their own side. They knew in the end—by 1940 all of them understood—that they had been attacked by something evil. They passed through the stage of defence and went on doggedly to finish the war so that they would not be attacked again. There are worse slogans than *Il faut en finir*[113] when people use it in a positive

112 the] omitted from 1st edn.
113 A phrase that Chamberlain used before Parliament, Sept. 1939, when he returned from secret discussions in France. Usually translated as 'It must be ended'.

sense. As attack broadened into victory, they began to formulate their beliefs more positively, to argue about peace, and the way men should live in a free world. But they had not needed anything as definite as this to conduct the war.

Another kind of belief altogether is needed to sustain men who are fighting. This latter belief has nothing to do with morality or the rights of nations, but is no more, in fact, than the organization of courage. All good armies, including the German, have this and when they lose it are no longer of any value.

Bravery is for most of us an acquired virtue. Many men can contemplate the idea of death with some philosophy. What is not so easy to contemplate is the physical effect of being torn in half by a shell. Modern war is deadly and impersonal and there is lacking very often the release of physical violence. Men have to walk forward under fire, quietly and in order, from one position to another, and no ordinary man enjoys this kind of thing.

The organization of courage comes from being part of a body of men who rely on each other and move together. This is what is called morale and has nothing to do with beliefs or speeches by politicians. Units of war who have this are unmistakable. It can be lost and regained. It needs at all times efficiency and a tightness of organization if it is to be held. You need to know when you go forward that others on your left and right are playing their part in a well-ordered plan. Their reliance on you, of which you are always conscious, gives you courage and strength and decision.

When old gentlemen talk about team-work, they are talking about morale in the same way but debasing it to a childish currency. The issues of war involve death, and death is rather more than an incident to the individual. This I remember being pointed out to a brigadier who offered bottles of beer for prisoners brought back on a raid; and[114] the men who were going on the raid swore quietly among themselves, feeling that the raid and their lives were something more than a game of darts. Only afterwards, coming back from the raid, they might talk about it as a game, and then only among themselves. Their actions in war were not thrown open to outsiders for comment.

There is a deep satisfaction for most men in this experience. In the complexity of life men live as individuals. If they are swept up together, it is in some mob emotion that leaves behind it a bitter taste. In war, when you are working well together, you find the sober pleasure of working in concert with friends and companions and at the same time feeling pride in yourself for the part which you can play as an individual. This takes place in war against a background of issues which are large enough to be impressed in your mind as life and death, and victory and defeat.

I believe this fact to be one reason why men are happy in wartime. Honest men know that war is to be fought and destroyed for the suffering and pain

114 and] omitted from 1st edn.

and crime that go with it. But honest men will also admit that they themselves as individuals have been happy in wartime and some of them have afterwards tried to find the same things in peace and always failed.

The system of mutual reliance, almost of love, which held men together in small fighting units during the war could be felt on a wider scale, but never consistently and never for long. It was a feeling not to be relied on but only to recognize with gratitude in its occasional glimpses. There came at times to each of us the realization that we were part of a movement that was as wide as the earth and a part of all humanity. This was a feeling that never came from words or speeches, but only at definite times and in the presence of material things, and probably cannot be recaptured now with words alone.

I remember coming on deck, a rough spring morning, north of the Irish coast, to see for the first time our convoy which had assembled overnight and was now steaming in formation out to the Atlantic. It was a large convoy for those days, which were still bad days on the oceans, though I know that there must have been many larger and more impressive gatherings of ships in the later invasion days. But to us then this convoy seemed like a meeting of all the famous ships we had known. They were all there, the Atlantic pleasure cruisers with famous names. There were two lovely ships of the Matson line that I remembered from the Pacific coming into Auckland years before, gleaming white, and that were now discoloured with grey camouflage but still good ships. Norwegian and Dutch ships, and freighters from the West Indies, and one ship of the old, much-loved, New Zealand line. Two great battleships of the Navy moved in the centre and smaller light cruisers and destroyers circled the outside so that whichever way you looked there seemed to be ships breaking the seas together, and you could feel then, not for the first or the last time, this warmth in being part of a great enterprise.

Some part of this feeling was dependent on the massing of armament and material power. When aeroplanes came in numbers to the desert fighting we saw for the first time, before Alamein, flights of Bostons, eighteen at a time, moving in perfect precision on a bombing mission and wheeling, their job done, and coming out again still intact and in order. Soldiers draw comfort from knowledge of the power that is behind them. They may be stirred by smaller, more individual sights, as we were once when three fighter planes came in to machine-gun German posts behind a ridge. There were emplacements there that we couldn't reach and from which we were mortared unpleasantly. The planes circled above us, almost lazily, fixing their target while enemy fire started to range on them, then dived, and we could watch dust and smoke kicking up from their fire along the rim of the ledge. They came over again and banked, as if ready to leave, while the sky round them was spattered with black puffs of anti-aircraft fire. The second time they came out, they were low on the ground and drawing small-arms fire all the way. Then they turned and came over again and I thought surely to God one of them will get hit this time, and began to pray mentally, the way you do trying to help a race-horse to come in. The third time they dived so low that they were out of sight behind the ridge and we counted them coming into sight again, the first two and then the third a long way behind but roaring along the ground and up into the sky again while the fire from every German gun in miles around seemed to be turned on them. But the three lovely Hurricanes were still untouched and went out of sight going home, coolly, flying together, with the air of men who have done a job well. You can be stirred and comforted in this way by the competence and bravery of other men when it is not on a large scale and not at all decisive in its results.

I remember again very clearly flying in to Greece. At that time, when Europe was still all Hitler's, there was a sombre reality in the *Festung Europa*.[115] In 1940 we had felt that perhaps we should never go in to Europe again or perhaps only after years of war in a later generation. There was a delight and inspiration now in going back to take part in the liberation. The pilots who took us in were young men and only rated as flight-sergeants. They had been working the Balkans for over a year, since the summer of 1942, taking supplies and men into Greece and Jugoslavia, as far east as Thrace and as far north as Tirna.

115 Lit. 'fortress Europe'. Hitler's plan to install a chain of fixed fortifications along the Western Front.

The work was hazardous rather than consistently dangerous. It called for skill in navigating and long minutes circling low among the mountains in bad weather searching for the pin-point of a signal flare, meeting sometimes night-fighters or flak coming back over the coast defences. They treated the job now[116] as a routine without romance. They ran to a schedule and knew the dropping-points as intimately as their aerodromes. There was not any need to talk with them or argue except to say at what height you would like them to run in for the jump, and then sit back in the plane going out at dusk over the Mediterranean, feeling yourself again part of an organization that was cool and efficient and would in the end break open the fortress of Europe without any need for speeches or writing or any further romanticism about the causes of the war.

We had a bad winter in Greece after that. There was civil war among the Greeks, some of whom thought the war was over. The Germans tightened their blockade around the mountains and burned villages so that the mountains were full of distressed and starving villagers and disarmed, barefooted Italians. We lived all through the winter with a group of partisans who were kind to us from native friendliness alone, since we had nothing to give them. No supplies came in. When aeroplanes were promised again we waited all through February and found each night snow and rain falling so that no plane could find us. We would go up at night from

116 now] omitted from 1st edn.

the village to a thatched shepherd's hut[117] on the mountain and wait there, crouched round a fire, for the sound of planes. The *andartes*[118] told stories and cursed the weather. Few of them had boots or proper clothes. They always laughed, promising each other new battledress, watertight boots, coffee, English cigarettes, when the planes came. One night a plane came overhead and circled trying to find us through the cloud, but mist thickened to rain and finally we could hear the plane flying away westward. Later in March a plane found us. The weather was still dirty with clouds blowing across the moon, but they saw our fires and came down, then lost them again before they could drop the stores. There were high peaks around there and the ground was dangerous. So we waited there in the mist and wind, listening to the drone of the plane above the cloud and knowing that they would not leave if possible without finding us again. We waited there for a quarter of an hour hearing the noise of the engine coming close and then disappearing, and thinking each time that perhaps it had been unable to stay and had left, until finally there was a brief rift in the clouds and out of them down on to the fires came this Halifax, like a friend, and dropped all its stores in two brief circles and then flashed its lamp in farewell. In better times and weather, later on, aeroplanes with stores were more

117 thatched shepherd's hut] 1st edn. revises to 'shepherd's thatched hut'.

118 Either a generic name for armed guerrillas, or more specifically Resistance groups associated with EAM/ELAS (see note 129 below).

commonplace. This first one was salvation. We knew
that we could be all right after this for a month or so
and could stop feeling like forgotten men.

Chapter Seven

These were some conclusions about war and its relation to belief. At the time I knew that there were deeper and unsolved questions of belief, of belief that is in the way men should live and how they should behave to one another. I reckoned that we would come back to these after the war. Meanwhile the English at least had enough in themselves to sustain them and enough aeroplanes to back them. In the spring of 1943, after Tunis, everyone was devoted to efficiency and to calculations as to how many Shermans would go on a Landing Craft, Tank. That was a period when no one worried any longer about war-aims, though some people started to worry about de Gaulle. But the Army that I knew then had found out that it was good and was busy with very practical matters. I reckoned that this practical approach to war would probably organize the Allies into Berlin sooner or later. If anyone had to be a soldier on that long hard road, the practical approach was probably as good as any and least subject to variation.

What became clear later on was that in winning the war by organization we had probably done little more than ensure for ourselves the comparative safety of 1939 and that we should have to start all over again and organize the peace. I suppose clear-minded political thinkers knew this all the time. My only conclusion, gained painfully, up to 1943 was that war-aims weren't necessary to battles, but that competence and material power were. God in fact was on the side of the big and the well-disciplined battalions. (Discipline, of course, is the wrong word since the wrong people always use it. If I use it here, it must imply not only an ability to obey orders, but all the friendliness and confidence that I have tried to describe.)

I knew also that you couldn't take any men from any country and organize them to prove this thesis. They had to be strong to begin with, possessed by a physical confidence in themselves. This was one of the breaks the English got in World War 2, a space of years to feed their half-starved millions so that you could see men grow from pallid and apologetic unemployed into soldiers. They had to have also a basic self-confidence in themselves as Englishmen. Some countries have martial traditions. (The English tradition used to be to distrust their generals but to feel that they can win the wars in spite of them.) Other countries have martial traditions which don't stand up very well to the objective gaze of history.

The Italians provided an interesting test-case. When we knew them briefly in the desert, they killed a lot of our friends—from a distance. It was significant that all their long-range weapons were excellent, their rifles, grenades, and bayonets wretched, and only when you got down[119] to sub-machine guns—useful for policing towns—did you find again reasonable workmanship.

When Italy surrendered, formally—a kind of indeterminate surrender had been going on for months—the Italians in Greece came over to us as to long-lost friends. All the Pinerolo division came over and the Duke of Aosta's cavalry, a rare fighting force that had ridden its splendid horses and burned villages on the Thessaly plain for over a year. They were beautifully dressed. An English officer of aristocratic tendencies remarked, 'How nice to deal with real soldiers again.' They had at least the uniforms.

They formed an ingenious compact with the Greek partisans, for whom their distaste was ill-concealed, by which they would not attack the Germans but would defend themselves if attacked. This was satisfactory to everybody. The Italian officers spent happy hours in the village cafes with us plotting lines on the map. They had the romantic conception of war by which if you draw a line on a map you have in some way created a defensive position. Their manners were excellent. They talked elegant French.

One might think slightly of their officers but no one could dislike the soldiers, not the young boys with their brown smiling faces. They rebuilt roads and houses which the Greeks, always averse to manual work, had never thought to touch. They shared the season's last grapes and sunshine with us

119 got down] 1st edn. has 'got them down'.

and made jokes about the Germans now occupying their barracks out on the plain. It was obvious that the Greek partisans would sooner or later disarm them: the contrast between the well-pressed uniforms and thick-soled boots of the Italians and the ragged, bare-footed partisans was too great. The Italians knew all this but made no effort to prevent it. Like the grass-hoppers of the fable they played in the sun and, when the day came and they were surrounded and disarmed, made no resistance but only complained afterwards tearfully.

A young liaison officer who worked with me daily came to tell me what happened. There had been no resistance, no bloodshed. 'These *andartes,*' he said, 'we spit on them. We would not soil ourselves by disputing with them if they want our arms.' He brooded morosely. 'What has this Mussolini done to us?' he said after a pause. 'We had a good Navy, a good Army; what for does the silly old bastard want to go to war?'

A month later the disarmed Italians had been stripped of their clothes and boots and were wandering the mountains. Rain began late in October and fell throughout November and after that the snows came down. German S.S. troops drove up through the foothills, burning villages and adding to the toll of refugees who took to the mountains.

When the Italians had come over to us they were commanded by three men of rank whom we watched with interest. The general of the Pinerolo[120] division

120 Pinerolo] typescript and 1st edn. both have 'Pinerole'.

had commanded the Ariete division at Alamein and, unlike this latter formation, had escaped to fight again. He spoke English, played a nice hand of bridge, and had political ambitions.[121] These ambitions he afterwards realized, since he managed to leave his men in Greece and make his way back to Italy where[122] he assumed a position of some importance. The other general, a kind of staff officer I never managed to place, was fat but, unlike many fat men, far from genial. From a breastful of medals he singled out for me, unasked, the campaign ribbons of Abyssinia, Spain, Albania. 'I have been in all campaigns,' he said, humourlessly oblivious of the fact that we might disapprove these wars. When the Germans attacked us in November, he hid up in the woods and went over to them. The third, a colonel, late commander of the cavalry, had an ugly reputation as a Fascist and burner of villages, also perhaps as executioner of hostages. He was thin, grey-haired, with a precise manner. I didn't reckon he would live long in Greek hands. He could have escaped to the Germans also but chose to stay with his men. When the snows came in November they started to die. We buried a thousand Italians in one melancholy area, which is a fair price to pay for Fascist glory. This colonel stayed with them all the time. I met him twice during that winter. The second time he was under

121 The commander of the Pinerolo division was General Adolfo Infanta (who later became ADC to Prince Umberto). The Ariete Division, one of the best Italian units in North Africa, was defeated by the New Zealanders in early July 1942.
122 realized, since he managed . . . where he assumed] 1st edn. revises to 'realized as, after his return to Italy, he assumed'.

arrest and the Greeks were starting to beat him up
as a preparation for trial. I don't know if he survived
or not. We tried to save him but lost touch with him.
He demonstrated to us that there might be admirable
qualities even in a Fascist, a simple truth perhaps, but
I expect he was just a good soldier who had learned
soldiering first under some man of quality.

Afterwards, the Italians who survived dispersed
into villages and worked their passage with the
villagers. Greek women, long ill-treated by their men,
grew very fond of them. They appreciated their good
manners and willingness to work. These women,
whose houses they had burned a year before, wept
when the time came to say good-bye to them.

Some joined us, as individuals, and were even
prepared to carry rifles when we went down to blow
up railway trains. They were good boys then, as loyal
and as brave and as subject to fear and fatigue as the
rest of us. If there are any conclusions to make about
Italians and war, it would be that they are a childish
people who should not incur such responsibilities. Like
children, they behaved cruelly when they had power
and, like children, they crumpled before anything
that seemed to them stronger than themselves. Not
the best discipline in the world nor the best arms
could make them into soldiers in any positive sense.
Only if they got away as individuals in some foreign
legion and stopped thinking of themselves as Italians,
a depressed people, could they become soldiers.

I guess any nation that grows up and makes
declarations and goes to war must take on the

responsibilities of an adult country, and the Italians paid a terrible price for their precocity. One positive result of this war may at least be chronicled, that I don't think the Italians will[123] come back to Greece for a long time, at least not as invaders.

123 that I don't think the Italians will] 1st edn. revises to 'the Italians won't'.

Chapter Eight

Most of us had gathered enlarged ideas of underground warfare. Journalists could be blamed for a good part of this since, like most literal people, they tend to grow romantic when, as happened in this case, they are deprived of all facts. They told stories about bearded partisans who took to the hills and held up German columns, or of others who loitered on street corners and knifed *carabinieri* as they passed. We ourselves were only too ready to believe most of what we read. It was heart-warming in the early days of the war to think of allies underground, not passive but active, and strangling the Germans over the breadth of Europe. I remember somebody wrote a book, *A Hundred Million Allies if We Want*,[124] from which it seemed that if the English declared for Socialism the war would be over in a few days. When John Steinbeck wrote *The Moon is Down* he was propounding a philosophy of resistance, but there was also a military idea in it—that, put crudely, if you handed out lumps of dynamite to enough people you could destroy the Germans. One way and another,

124 I have not been able to identify any book of that title.

we must have handed out quite a lot of dynamite in Europe, along with Sten guns, pistols, and hand-grenades, but historians will probably agree that the Germans were beaten first on the main fighting fronts.

Greeks and Englishmen were working in Greece from 1941 onwards. By the time we came to go there in the late summer of 1943, they had set up an organization which removed most of the excitement and danger from one's entry. Personally I always found parachuting unpleasant in its physical sensations, but beyond that we couldn't pride ourselves on doing anything very extraordinary. The partisans controlled most of mountain Greece by then and it was simply a matter of jumping out of the aeroplane at the right place.

Yet there was a queerness and oddness about the situation all the same, something abnormal in wandering round freely in an enemy-held country, so that one could retain a sense of adventure even when there was no danger. I knew a man who spent nine months in Greece and went out by *caïque* from the coast of Pelion and in all that time never saw a German. He was perhaps a little less adventurous than most. I don't imagine he went out of his way to look for Germans, and indeed his superiors asked him when he got out of Greece what he had been supposedly[125] doing all those nine months, but there wasn't anything very exceptional about his experience.[126]

125 been supposedly] 1st edn. revises to 'supposedly been'.
126 experience] 1st edn. has 'experiences'.

The day we arrived in Trikala, up in the north-west corner of Thessaly, the Italians were moving up into the hills to join the partisans, and the Germans were moving up into Trikala to take over the town. In the confusion and excitement we nearly found ourselves left there to meet them, but met instead a middle-aged Greek who claimed to be a general and sat with him on a shadeless hill over Trikala watching the German column move along the road. I knew no Greek then and anyway found the military situation so strange as to be not possibly affected by any remarks of mine.

This was the first time that I saw the plains of Thessaly that I afterwards came to know and love so well. They stretched out flat, like a desert, only very green and rich in the sunlight. There were mountains all round them that jutted out like cliffs into a sea of green cornfields. On a clear day, like this one, you could look across to Olympus and south of it to those other fine, symmetrical mountains—Ossa (that men now call Kissavos), Mavrovouni, and Pelion. South of the plain were the low ranges of Othris and the lesser Mavrovouni, and all round the rest of the plain the twisted ranges of the Pindus, rugged and tortured, as if they had been created in bad temper.

After the Italians left, the Germans moved in with swift mastery and took over all the plain. They garrisoned the main roads and the railway lines and stayed in the small market towns. All the rest was free Greece where men could wander in uniform and hold parades and make speeches (which latter[127] turned out to be a favourite occupation).

Later that same afternoon, we drove across the plain to the little burned village of Porta. It had been burned in the spring by the Italians, those same Italians who were now coming over to fight for freedom and democracy, or anything else the men on top told them was worth fighting for. Now there were only about four houses standing in Porta. The rest was blackened walls and tumbled masonry. There was an alfresco café working on the ruins of what had once been a village shop. We sat at the salvaged tables and the conference resumed itself. Into the single street of the village poured bearded *andartes,* well-dressed Italians, the loaded mules of fleeing civilians. In the end it was night-time and we were still sitting there. News came in but no one cared much for it. The Germans drove into Trikala. The Italians moved two armoured cars down the road to give us protection. *Andartes* took up positions on[128] the forward hills. The cafe owner brought out *ouzo,* which is a sombre drink, cousin to absinthe and *arrak.* He also had bread and sliced tomatoes. A small child, I guess about five years old, walked round the tables chanting, 'EAM-ELAS—the people's rule'.[129] As with most Greeks, politics was to be his alphabet. A husky fellow with a dilapidated

127 latter] omitted from 1st edn.
128 on] 1st edn. has 'in'.
129 Acronym for Ethnikón Apeleftherikón Métopon-Ethnikós Laikós Apeleftherikós Stratós, the National Liberation Front resistance movement and its military wing, the National Popular Liberation Army.

cowboy hat stationed himself by the road-side with a pot of paint. He was making all the Italian trucks stop as they came through, and was daubing them with slogans of the 'people's rule'. The Italians were not liking this very much, mainly because it spoiled the smartness of their well-kept trucks, but you could see the comrade with the paint-pot reckoned himself to be on work of national importance. Greeks began singing. They were happy then, with the Italian surrender, as if they had won a victory. Their bearded faces nodded in the light of a single oil-lamp as they sang. There was lament as well as hope in the songs that they sang; they were in a tradition and cadence that ran back through centuries of Turkish slavery. I went to sleep in the end while they were still singing.

All of this was partisan warfare as one might have hoped to find it, friendly, and picturesque, and a little comic, and perhaps not very practical. I would like[130] in many ways to have had[131] it stay like that, but we were soldiers then, even if only amateurs, and so concerned ourselves with military matters.

We moved back into the hills behind Kalambaka to a partisan headquarters and spent a lot of time studying dispositions on the map and more time arguing as to who would feed our new Italian allies. The weather stayed warm and mild and the sun kept shining into October. There was no war anywhere. One day the Germans moved up to Kalambaka and fired a few shots and went back again, so this was a

130 like] 1st edn. has 'have liked'.
131 had] omitted from 1st edn.

victory. We started to buy in dried food and cognac for the winter.

Early in October the Greeks started a civil war, the big party against the small, but all the fighting was over the mountains in Epirus and did not disturb us. A little later our comrades disarmed the Italians and this caused some complications which can best be classed as administrative. Rain fell for a few days and then cleared again. Life was very comfortable and friendly in the village. Just after that, towards the end of October, the Germans collected a force and moved up towards us in the hills.

Nothing up till then had helped me to[132] think seriously of war in this setting. There was so pleasant an air of live and let live about Greece that I couldn't imagine anyone being wanton enough to disturb us.

From Kastania, where we were living, a motor road, winding and difficult, went down to Kalambaka. From the hill-side above the village you could look down this road to the valley above Kalambaka where we had first landed. The *andarte* lines of defence were a long way below where the road from Kalambaka narrowed into a pass above the town. We had artillery and machine-guns, battalions of men, and even a telephone line connecting us with the fighting front. I never saw any of this except on a map, and one of the guns afterwards and a few of the *andartes,* but this is the way it looked from the village of Kastania up in the hills in that late October sunshine.

The small mountain villages of Greece have an

132 me to] typescript has 'to to'.

economy that is very self-contained. In small cleared patches among the pine forests they work with wooden ploughs and oxen and grow for themselves meagre crops of wheat and maize. They harvest wheat in June and maize in September and store it carefully for the winter, which is long, snowbound, and bitter. Each household keeps a few goats, the richer ones run flocks of sheep. These give them milk and cheese in the spring months, wool which they weave themselves into thick, warm blankets and clothing, and even soft leather for slippers or saddlery when the markets are denied to them. Eggs, chicken, and meat are luxuries for saints' days and Christmas-time. Wine and *ouzo* are luxuries too, but each house manages a little for party times. Dried beans and lentils are the last necessities and olive oil which has to be bought in by trade. This is a close economy which gives survival and not too bad a time, in good seasons, but a plague of locusts or a snow-storm in May, or a war, means disruption and then people start to die, first the very old and the very young and the sick, and after that the ordinary strong peasant men and women also die.

The villages and the houses in them all have much of a pattern. They are built on the steeply shelving sides of hills, stone houses, often with two floors, the bottom floor being for goats and mules and other items of capital. The houses are crowded closely together and have rough stone paths twisting in and out of them to village springs which run all through the summer with clear and beautiful water of which the Greeks are very proud. There will sometimes

be only fifty and sometimes two hundred houses in
a village. Most of the houses are very old, the best
of them built in Turkish days. They are not very
beautiful nor sanitary, but they give homes to people
who only know this kind of life and who, in good
times, have been not[133] unhappy in it. A lot of these
villages are burned now. In some of these villages,
those who did the burning went round afterwards
and blew in the stone walls, so that all you would see
now visiting them is a huddle of stone and masonry,
just like the villages in fact where the really big and
important fighting has taken place on the main fronts
of Europe.

Sitting in Kastania in October we heard the sound
of firing on the first day and went round from time to
time to get news of the battle. There, at headquarters,
we had big maps, dispositions, flags, and we talked
leisurely about the battle, the war, the civil war. There
did not seem to be any news of the battle except that
everything was all right, and then the next morning
there was not any front, no guns, no battalions, no
artillery, and the Germans were fifteen miles below
us doing a little practice shooting round the hills, just
to let everyone know that they were coming on and to
warn everyone to stand back.

The Germans were very leisurely in their
advance that day. They had villages to burn and took
their time moving[134] up the road. There was no firing
and we could watch the smoke from farm-houses

133 been not] 1st edn. has 'not been'.
134 moving] 1st edn. has 'driving'.

and villages rolling up into the blue sky. *Andartes* came back through the villages and went on into the hills. They brought with them a lot of mules and one gun—the other gun had been abandoned. I still did not understand that there was not going to be any fighting and that we were all going away and merely leaving the village and the people in it to make the best peace they could with the Germans. One of our friends from the village came round to offer us mules if we wanted to move out, but this was in the morning and we thought then the example would be bad if we left. By the afternoon I realized that we needn't have worried, for by then all the maps and flags in the headquarters had been packed up and shifted out and the general, riding off on a horse, told me where I could find him in two days' time. By that time there weren't any mules to be found, since the people of the village were using them all to move their stores out into the hills.

I saw afterwards many times in Greece the same sad spectacle of men and women and children fleeing from their homes, but it never failed to move me with a sense of tragedy and waste. All through that night the village was noisy with the tinkling bells of animals on the move and babies crying and women calling to their children.

At headquarters, now bare and empty, a single frightened-looking officer sat on duty. A more sturdy telephonist kept communication back into the hills behind. 'I will stay here,' he told us, 'it is a small thing to die for one's country.' He told us also that a

gallant rearguard down on the road below us, outside
the village, would also die for their country so that
at all events we would hear shooting if the Germans
came and would have warning. I told them that when
the shooting started we would go down and join the
rearguard, but as a precaution one of our party went
down and blew a hole in the road. He came back early
in the morning to say that there wasn't any rearguard
and by that time the frightened officer and the sturdy
telephonist had also gone and the village was empty
except for a few old women who presumably didn't
care whether they lived or died. Later that morning
we sat in the trees above the village and watched
the Germans, who had by now repaired the hole we
had blown, move up along the road. They moved
with the easy precision of a trained advance guard.
Nobody fired at them. When they got to the village
they fired on people and sheep that could still be seen
running up into the shelter of the trees. They sent
motorcyclists along the clay track to the next village
where they captured our half-evacuated wireless set,
several thousand dollars' worth of paper money, and
all the winter clothing and cognac we had so carefully
stored. Personally I set out to keep my rendezvous
with the general. He had set it for two days' time and
the place was two days travelling away, back and in
among the mountains. Odd houses on the edge of
Kastania started to burn.

The Germans spent several days in and around
Kastania. I never went back there but I heard all
about it. They sent parties up into the hills and called

to the village people who were hiding out there to come down. If they saw anyone trying to run away they shot at them. One way and another they killed quite a few people and also a good many animals. Those who came down into the village they locked up in the church and kept them there until they had finished with the village. Then they let them go but there was no longer any village to go back to. They burned several villages in that area, all those that could be reached easily and without too much trouble, carrying petrol and incendiary grenades. They were very smart boys these,[135] S.S. troops for the most part and quite young, and very efficient, not only in fighting—for which they had no immediate call—but also in reprisals and incendiarism.

During the next month of November and into December it seemed to me that villages were burning all over Greece. The Germans drove through along the Metsovo-Janina road. After that they came in to Karpenisi and up from Agrinion. The Greeks kept fighting each other in the west. In late November we crossed to Pelion for purposes of negotiation and found Germans raiding in above Volos. When we came back across the Thessaly plain, we waited two days for a safe crossing of the main north road and railway line and, as we waited, saw a line of fires burning along the western edge of the plain. When December began and brought the first heavy snows, free Greece, partisan, *andarte* Greece, was marked by a boundary of blackened villages, its territory

135 these] omitted from 1st edn.

determined by a host of starving refugees. This was the way things were when the winter began, the last, black winter of 1943.

We had a good deal of time for consideration during that winter. Politics and the Greek civil war had determined for us a virtual blockade of the Greek partisans; but we lived with them in Thessaly in complete friendliness. If Costa Tsamakos should survive to read this,[136] which I doubt, for his opinions are well known and outspoken, I hope he will still remember our friendship and the long snow-bound hours when we cheered each other in Fourna, passing *tsippouro*—a lower-class cousin of *ouzo*—across the fire and exchanging reminiscences. He was a grey-haired old general of the Venizelos era whose decorations reached back to the Salonika campaign. I never spoke to him frankly all that passed in my mind then about the worthlessness of his partisans, but we had a great friendship and I think I promised him that if I ever grew to sufficient stature to publish my reminiscences, an unlikely contingency, his photograph, which I still possess, would adorn it.

It would be untrue to say that in all the attacks and depredations which had been conducted by the Germans, our *andartes* had offered no resistance or defence, but the resistance was of a formal kind. It consisted so often of a few scattered shots fired from a distance, followed by an inevitable and hurried retreat. The Germans went where they wanted to go. If they

136 On Mulgan's relationship with Tsamakos (who did survive), see *Long Journey to the Border* (282 et seq.).

had any casualties, they must have been from motor accidents on the mountain roads. Their purpose was clear in all this burning. They wanted to break the resistance movement by starving out the mountains, and also by showing the people that their *andartes* were worthless and offered them no protection. In a more complex civilization this might have succeeded. But the villagers, once they understood what was happening, hid their stores of grain and flocks in the hills and waited until the enemy had gone, and then moved back again into the ruins of their houses. What hatred they felt continued to be concentrated on the Germans who had burned their houses. Towards their own fighting men who had brought this on them they felt perhaps apathy and showed despair, but never hostility.

The real heroes of the Greek war of resistance were the common people of the hills. It was on them, with their bitter, uncomplaining endurance, that the German terror broke. They produced no traitors. We moved freely among them and were guided by them into German-held villages by night without fear. They never surrendered or compromised, and as a result the Germans kept five divisions guarding Greece all through the war. The Greek people paid a terrible and disproportionate price for this resistance. When people speak slightingly of Greeks and of their way-wardness and foolishness in fighting each other, there is some point in remembering these things.

But we were soldiers then and had to keep remind-ing ourselves of it, the way I keep repeating it here, and were puzzled and a little ashamed to find ourselves working with a resistance movement that never did any fighting. Some said angrily that all Greeks were cowards. Others, that only Greeks of one political persuasion had any military value, that the rest took arms for political power and not to fight Germans. Myself, I doubted the truth of either thesis.

I knew that in the early days of the movement, when the first Greeks went into the hills, they had done brave and remarkable things. Since then too many men had given up comfortable homes and families and gone into the hills, too many men and of too diverse a kind to be drawn by any simple political belief.

Somehow, it seemed to me, the movement had outgrown itself and become militarily worthless. At some stage, Greek army officers, whose sense of dignity and grandeur outweighed their intelligence, had made a movement which should have been small, compact, and irregular in design, into a vast army. They spoke now of divisions, regiments, and battalions, first, second, and third bureaux. With this went all the trappings and organization of regular warfare, but they lacked, of course, those things that are necessary to regular war, like a system of supply, proper arms, and a uniform, tested corps of officers and men. They had nothing but contempt for the small, personally led bands with which the movement had started. Their new army gave them a sense of dignity and status; the fact that it was of no military value didn't strike them.

The Greeks, like all nations, have certain faults, and one of them is a sublime inability to take advice. They were hurt when we gently hinted that their men never did any fighting. They always had tales to tell us of heroism and casualties inflicted on the enemy and believed these stories. The battles always took place some way away or some time before; it was the height of bad manners to try and check up on one of these battles. None of these leaders looked with eyes of realism. So many times they would show us lines and flags of positions on a map and then you would go down to this fighting front and find perhaps ten men crouched round a fire and a watch being kept for them by a small boy at the far end of the village, and all of them packed ready to go if the enemy came.

Chapter Nine

Winter settled down over Greece. The first snows came in early December but the real snows began in January and ran through February and March. 'We have seven falls of snow in the mountains,' an old man told me. I lost count in the end but there were a good deal[137] more than seven. Snow lay thickly under the pine-trees and made travelling with mules or horses impossible. 'Call out the women,' the village president would say if we had stores to shift. I could never get used to this habit of treating women as not very valuable animals, but I could see the advantages of the system and only look forward with sardonic longing to the day when women get the vote in Greece.

We did a lot of travelling that winter in spite of the snow. By January the Germans had burned all the easily accessible villages and had settled down to wait for the spring before they started again. There was no fighting, so we travelled, trying to organize relief for the homeless and destitute. The only kind of relief that we had to offer was gold sovereigns, which at least acted as a kind of channel for bringing wheat from

137 deal] 1st edn. has 'many'.

the plains up into the hills. You couldn't eat gold sovereigns, of course, but, nevertheless, if you were lucky you might buy something with them. The comrades accused us of trying to corrupt the country with 'yellow fever' and they may have been right. I know that I felt the inadequacy of what we were doing, each time that we went into some ruined village and talked to the people, and watched young children lying sick without medicines, or old men trying to patch up mud roofs to keep out the cold and rain.

We crossed the plain of Thessaly, from the Pindus by Kharditsa, across by Dhomokhos and over Othris to Pelion many times. Those were journeys that can be remembered now not only for cold and discomfort. There was little danger. Guides from each village would come out at night and take us over the railway line between the guards and patrols, which were infrequent then. Crossing the line we would see flares going up from lonely garrisons and hear sometimes shots fired questingly into the night, but for the most part the country was peaceful and was ours to move in. But I remember, personally, more than any of these things, and more than long hours of silent travel, and the deep mud of the Thessaly plain and the eight feet of snow that turned us back over Stenoma, more than these, faces of people that came out of their houses in the small hours of the night to welcome us and take us in and feed us and guide us.

The first journey that we made, before the winter set in, we were carrying gold to Pelion and came to a small village above Dhoxara and arriving[138] there, above the guarded railway line, with dawn just breaking, had people woken[139] up to give us beds; and when we got up again three hours later, there was hot milk and fresh eggs and bread for us before we moved on. There was a little man there, the village schoolmaster, who organized it all. He had a wizened, small face, and kept making jokes that I couldn't understand. I remember him and his mother also, who was still quite fresh and happy at something over seventy years of age. In April of the next year, someone blew up a German troop train just below the village, and the Germans, being practical people, took seventeen men from the village and shot them by the railway line. The only one whose name I knew on the list was the little schoolmaster, but I expect there were others from among those that we had met who had been kind to us. It wasn't a very big village.

Other times and places of the same kind remain, fires by night when all the family, sleeping in one room, would wake up and move over, the small children crying and being hushed to sleep again, so that we could get near the fire and get dry. The old woman in Vardhali who came out to see some Englishmen, the first she had seen since 1941; the old man in Makrakomi whose house had been twice burned by Germans, and whom we found building a shelter of stone and thatch. 'I'll fool them this time,' he told us slyly, 'I'm going to build it small.'

138 arriving] 1st edn. has 'on our arrival'.
139 had people woken] 1st edn. has 'people were woken'.

I had a long ride by myself in late August of 1944, in the dying summer when the Germans were already starting to leave. When the moon went down I was still a long way from home, and stopped by a shepherd's fire for the night. We shared an American 'K' ration which seemed to this friendly fellow the acme of modern science, not least the small packet of ersatz coffee which we cooked over his fire, and the five Chelsea cigarettes. We didn't talk about the war, or all the villages that the Germans had destroyed in a last, savage drive that August, or about politics, which takes precedence over weather for social occasions in Greece, but about farming, and how he was going to get back to his land on the edge of the plain now that the Germans were going, and what seeds he would plant and the programme for winter ploughing. We made coffee again before dawn and separated before either of us could see the other clearly in daylight, but if we met again would[140] know each other and, I guess, could go on talking about farming very happily.

There was some quality in these people, as there is, I expect, in all simple peasant people, that was solid and indestructible. You could forgive them all the times that they double-crossed you over the sale of a mule or argued with dull obstinacy for some course of action that was clearly absurd, and still be proud to know them and more proud if you felt that[141] they liked you.

In all the troubles and political difficulties that

140 would] 1st edn. has 'we would'.
141 that] omitted from 1st edn.

came to us in Greece, I often wondered how we would have felt in occupied England if the Americans had come in to us with golden dollars and arms to lead our resistance movement, and just how politely we would have reacted to their direction.

In April the snow thawed on Timfristos. We passed Easter in sunshine and with wine, making plans for the last summer of the war in Greece. We were simple fellows then and concerned with fighting Germans. I can see of course, now,[142] that this was a mistake and feel a kind of vacuum now that this straightforward and precise objective has been removed. A lot of Greeks with whom we were working had diverse and varying objectives. We took the line then that it wasn't our business to unravel the thoughts that lay behind their actions, but only to use them when they coalesced against the Germans. As a policy, and within my own small sphere, this worked[143] not badly. I had grown up myself to think of German Fascism as so bad and big an evil that anything against it must have some element of good, and still believe that while perhaps our simplicity was a mistake, the evils that have been left us as a legacy are themselves a part of that same anarchic order of Europe which the Germans introduced.

We tried to make changes in a purely military way so that some heart could go back into the resistance movement. It was too late to break down the fantastic order of divisions. Too many Greek staff officers, who

142 of course, now,] 1st edn. has 'now, of course'.
143 worked] 1st edn. has 'worked out'.

lived back in the mountains and issued counter-orders to one another, would have become unemployed. But we tried to attach to ourselves a small group of men who would do the work, inside this wasteful framework.

Orde Wingate[144] laid down some principles of irregular warfare, and I don't suppose the War Office will ever lean heavily on what endorsement I give them here. But he said in particular that there must be some hard core of troops from outside the movement who could, if necessary, do something by themselves. With even a small number of men who will stay, and keep order and discipline, one is never helpless; and, most of all in argument, there always comes a time when you have to say that this thing, if necessary, you will do by yourselves. One man saying this in a military argument is usually no more than a romantic, but two men saying it and standing by each other begin to have some effect, and if you have twenty men who always take orders, you have in your hands the beginning of a movement.

Wingate said: 'Never ask favours, but tell people if they care to help they can come along, that you yourself are going anyway.'

We started first, in the spring of 1944, with a group of Polish boys who had deserted from the Germans and volunteered to stay with us. They were

144 Wingate was a British Army officer who created special military units in Palestine in the 1930s, and in Burma in WW2. Unorthodox in his methods, he is admired by some as a brilliant tactician in guerilla warfare, but others see him as a fanatic, guilty of considerable brutality.

heartbreakingly young and had the nonchalance of all Poles in this war who look forward to no certain future or homecoming, no wives, no families, no homeland, and only an idea. Everything that has happened to the Poles in this war has combined to make them a little crazy. They were always romanticists, and now the romance of this idea of Poland is about all they have left. This quality doesn't make them any less attractive nor any less good as soldiers. They have discipline and a kind of gallantry among themselves. These boys had been drafted out of Germany, on compulsion, to save their families. They ran away when they got to Greece. The comrades, however, never trusted them, labelled them Fascists with that smooth facility which is the mark of our age, and disliked them because they refused to take part in the civil wars of Greece. They served us well, but the dislike which the comrades felt for them stayed with them and hindered them.

As the summer came in, American and British commando troops joined us. They made journeys that would be epic in peacetime from west to east of Greece. Mule trains from the villages ferried their stores and arms. There were not many of them but they supplied what was needed in distinctiveness, in the feeling that they brought of being a part of the united nations,[145] the same glow that a rare marauding

145 united nations] 1st edn. capitalizes as 'United Nations'. Mulgan is
    presumably thinking of the 1942 agreement forged by Churchill
    and Roosevelt in which twenty six Allied nations pledged, in what
    was called the 'Declaration by United Nations', to continue fighting
    the Axis Powers.

aircraft could give us diving over the mountains to shoot up the railway line.

Seeing English soldiers again, I knew how much affection people like myself who were not really English had in us for the English people. They brought with them an entire fragment of the British army, in language and jokes and manners. There was something unassimilable about them, so that the Greeks liked them but always stayed at a distance, and three English soldiers sitting by a village fountain talked among themselves as if they were still in England, while the villagers grouped themselves round them in a circle, friendly and observant, ready to make the first approaches which were not rejected but somehow disregarded.

The Americans were more glamorous. They had the best equipment in the world and an air, in carrying it, that made them look like a film-director's design for commando troops. All their vocabulary of war had the same picturesque toughness. A nice thing about living with them was that they included you in it. There was a friendly generosity about their outlook on life, that assumed to start with that you must be the hell of a fine fellow, and it didn't take long for you to inherit this splendid conviction yourself. Part of it was a camouflage, a sort of dressing that they had for the world and particularly for the ugly business of war, a way that they had of helping each other along; but it seemed to me as good as most. It may be time to stop when it gets into cigarette advertisements and the *Reader's Digest*, with capital letters, calling itself The

American Way of Life. But for war, in comradeship
and naturalness, it deserves all commendation.

By April, when we reorganized ourselves, and
more so by the summer, when all these others arrived,
we had got back to some kind of military activity that
made partial sense. Small numbers of partisans, never
more than a hundred in all, had been allotted to us.
We lived with them and travelled with them and what
fighting we did was done with them. I think we grew
to respect each other. In wartime everything shared is
a bond. In error—and trial—you sort out the people
that you know you can trust and that will stay with
you. After a short time, every danger, every journey
that you have endured together provides so much the
more element for humour and conversation. I think
the comrades who directed partisan policy from
somewhere back in the hills suspected the friendship
which grew up between us. I don't know what they
thought we were doing in the hours when we walked or
rode or sat round fires and talked together: laying plans
for a capitalist counter-revolution perhaps. I know, at
least, that they would have found our conversation
harmless and a little trivial, like all soldiers' gossip,
concerned with our wives and children, and with jokes
about how[146] one had tripped on a sleeper trying to
lay charges quietly on the railway line, or how another
had mistaken one of us for a German and fired wildly
with the fortunate ill success that attends all shooting
at night. I know that our knowledge of colloquial
Greek improved, often on the seamy side, and that

146 jokes about how] typescript has 'jokes how'.

corruption may have set in on happy occasions when we celebrated something that we thought had been worth doing by buying drink and a sheep from the village and declaring a feast for ourselves.

The village of Palaia Yannitsou will probably never be very famous in history. It lies, or stands—for it is perched high and is draughty in winter—on the southern border of Thessaly. You can still see heaped stones there that mark the old Turkish boundary. New Yannitsou is an hour's walk down the hill-side towards Lamia. Old Yannitsou is the remnants of a village, no more than thirty ramshackle houses, with one good spring for water that surprisingly never dried in summer, and an old priest and a committee of village elders that would be jailed on sight in any more sophisticated community. From Old Yannitsou you could see the curving railway line above Lamia, and the German guards at Kastri, and the full sweep of the Sperkheios valley, and Timfristos, and Giona, and, on a clear day, Pelion and Olympus. When we left there and said good-bye and paid all our bills in British sovereigns—no mere ceremony this latter— they said that they would never forget us, and I believe this to be true, for we had many things to remember in common from the months that we spent there.

Partisan warfare is puny in its standards and puny in results, but you get somehow a disproportionate satisfaction from it. No great skill is needed to lay explosive charges on a railway line, no great danger attends the party that lies up and fires on a wrecked train. Merely to be operating there enlarged the satisfaction, to know that this one corner at least was not entirely *Festung Europa*. The satisfaction might be dimmed by seeing a village burning in reprisal the next morning, or getting a list of killed hostages 'for information and return'.

Greeks have a happy disregard of human life in the abstract. I was a little shocked in the first month I spent in Greece, watching the casual execution by the partisans of fifteen unhappy Vlachs who had been persuaded by Italian propaganda into believing that they were the heirs to a Roman empire in the mountains of Greece. They were condemned to death by the partisans and led out on a fine, sunny afternoon in September. Small children stood around watching and village mothers paused in an afternoon walk to see what happened. They were shot down by two men with Sten guns and piled in one heap into a common grave. I didn't notice anyone saddened or shocked, or that life in Kastania ran less uneventfully that evening.

For ourselves, as we worked through the summer of 1944, the bill seemed to run higher. Each good Greek dead I would rate as a debit against the Ministry of Economic Warfare[147] who employed us. How many hanged hostages balance the enemy's loss of a wrecked locomotive? The ideal partisan is inspired by some belief that does not rate itself in terms of human life. When he fights an enemy as methodical and skilful as the German, he knows that his country will pay dearly and mortgage more than one generation for victory in our time.

147 of Economic Warfare] omitted from 1st edn.

By late July we knew that we had earned a more than common retribution, and reports of S.S. troops gathering in Lamia told us that it was near at hand. They drove in below us, and the fabric of partisan divisions collapsed as it always had and would collapse.[148] From Old Yannitsou we did some sporadic shooting, but the Germans were engaged on reprisal and concerned themselves little with military objectives that involved clearing us back from the railway line. They knew well enough that they were leaving. Three years before, in the triumphant days of the Wehrmacht, a young German officer had saluted his Führer from the Acropolis. The same young officer, perhaps a little dimmed, was now packing up to go. But they had in mind to leave some mark upon Greece, a memorial perhaps less durable than the Acropolis but enough to see out a generation or two. We watched the villages burning from Yannitsou. I could list their names here; there were more than forty of them, but they would not mean anything and are only nice-sounding and friendly places to remember now that they no longer exist. For this burning had a certain final Germanic thoroughness. In all those villages no houses were left. Those that did not burn adequately were dynamited. For a week we watched smoke rising over the Sperkheios valley. It rolled up thickly and blotted out Giona from our view. Terrified villagers crowded into the hills and huddled by night round camp-fires, cherishing the

---

148 always had and would collapse] 1st edn. has 'always had collapsed and always would'.

few pathetic belongings that they had rescued. Part of all this was in a tradition of ancient and oriental days when conquerors marked their marches with fire and sword. Not much of it, in the wildest perspective, belonged to the modern world.

I don't know accurately how many people were killed during this last German drive. Of[149] reliable evidence I would cite a survivor from Makrokomi, who was one of twenty hostages held there when the trucks first rolled up from Lamia. They were passing the time well enough with their German guards until a truck came back with ten German dead who had been unlucky enough to run into partisan resistance. When this happened the twenty hostages were put up against a wall and shot, and this one survivor, bearing his evidence in a thigh wound, came away. I saw the bodies of two old women and one old man that I had known, shot and not killed and left to burn in the baths, the pleasure resort of Platistomo. Happy days, I guess, all over Europe. Atrocity no longer wears a frightening aspect. We are hardened now and take these things as something natural that is to be expected when great nations go to war. I even feel something of shame writing about them, but would feel perhaps more ashamed if I did not write down these things, remembering these people and refusing to set down their story, merely because it is commonplace.

One needed to be of rather less than average sensibility to take pleasure in sabotage exploits against this background. If you meet in after days men who

149 Of] 1st edn. has 'As'.

pride themselves on partisan exploits, question them
a little more closely on the matter of reprisals and
the danger which they themselves incurred. Myself, I
remember of many times going down to the railway
line on some far from desperate project, the look on
the faces of peasant women who, knowing we were
working there and that reprisals would follow, were
loading the family donkeys with what they thought
might be saved from the wrath to come. I remember,
too, the people of Kaitsa, which is a little village lying
alongside the railway between Lamia and Dhomokhos.
Their village was burned first by the Italians in the
summer of 1943 and again for good measure in the
autumn of the same year. All the time that I knew
them they lived in thatched *kalivis* above the village.
These straw huts are fine in good weather and very
romantic in pictures, but bad for children and invalids
when there is snow on the ground. When we started
to operate again in 1944 above Kaitsa, they sent a
deputation to us. The priest who led it was a friend
and as smooth a politician as you could care to meet.
The villagers who came with him were saddened and
hardened. They had the look of all peasant Greeks,
of men who don't expect much fun but are prepared
to endure. They didn't ask us to stop sabotaging the
railway line, but requested modestly that if we did
anything it would be on a scale comparate[150] to the
reprisals that would follow.

People make jokes about the Greeks and I know
that much bitterness came afterwards, as is inevitable

150 scale comparate] typescript has 'comparate scale'.

with civil war, but few of those whom I heard criticizing them are competent to judge. I would take comments, and I know the villagers of Kaitsa would take them, from Londoners or Czechs or front-line soldiers in the campaign of the last winter of the war, but not from anyone else and not from exiled governments living abroad in comfort.

In late October we rode down into Lamia, the day that the Germans left. Along the road, through blackened villages, people came out to hang flowers on the mule saddles. They offered us drinks and sweet cakes. There is always a thrill and satisfaction in penetrating the enemy line after his retreat, in seeing at first hand the trenches and defences that you have studied for so long from a distance. The railway line, wrecked by both sides and now derelict, seemed a paltry objective. It was hard to understand that these concrete pill-boxes had kept a free people in subjection. People were happy and Greece was free. As we rode down, the last German trucks were still visible, winding up the road to Derven Fourka above Lamia. But victory had come to a tired and an old and a weary people. The road we travelled was lined with graves that we could not see, and for each person that shook us by the hand we could imagine a son or a brother who should have been there to shelter us from reproach, and was not there—being dead.

Chapter Ten[151]

When I was young, and particularly in university days, I seem to remember that there were a great many books available on the 'theory' of Communism, but I do not recollect many text-books on the more important subject of its practice; that is, on how to start a revolutionary party and on how to control it once you have got the party started. I don't know if I have been able to explain adequately the idealism that we had felt as young men for the Communist party, or perhaps more generally for the socialist theories of the Left. It was they who had fought and they alone who offered something of a future, a programme for builders. There has always seemed to me something basically wrong with young men who grow up in comfortable circumstances and cheerfully accept the conservatism of an older generation. I rate lower still, but perhaps more from prejudice than proper knowledge, those young men who disguise their conservatism behind a facade of committees, who protest in the name of Disraeli the politics of radical Toryism, the young men who do not want anything

151 Ten] misnumbered as 'XI' in autograph addition to typescript.

changed—least of all their own security—but are anxious to remove from conservatism the stigma of intransigence.

But later in life, and under the duress of war, we were subjected to rather more searching tests in matters of politics. The Communists we met in Greece were not working on any yellow-backed, Left-Book-Club manual. They were practical fellows and inclined to argue by results—pragmatists, I suppose you might call them. They were the cause of concern to us and something of a readjustment[152] in our political thinking.

Communism in Greece would necessarily be something of an anomaly. Lenin devoted a few words to Spain, which is a similar country in its mountains and bare, peasant economy, but very different from Greece in being saddled with an aristocracy and a politically minded Church. The Greeks have no aristocracy, except the fellows who have made good with a fish-shop in America and come home to spend their money. Their religion is a straightforward affair, of superstition rather than belief, and their priests are simple men who marry and have children and go left or right in politics according to popular tendencies. All Greeks are individualists and intensely interested in their own possessions. There are few factories in Greece and nothing that could be technically described as a proletariat, though there are a lot of poor people, who are poor mainly because the

152 something of a readjustment] typescript has 'something of readjustment'; 1st edn. has 'of some readjustment'.

country is poor and because it has been lived in for a long time and denuded. There are a few rich people in Greece, but they are mostly merchants, who might as well be in Greece as anywhere else, Levantines and internationalists, people with a home and a passport in Syria or Egypt and a flat in Kolonaki for just so long as the political temperature is favourable.

Some element of Communism might be made suitable to Greece, but it would have to be of a very co-operative and democratic nature to last. The plains of Thessaly and Macedonia and Agrinion would work well as co-operatives, with pooled machinery and marketing. There is a good deal of co-operative law and custom already in the villages,[153] agreement as to grazing rights and forestry, rules for the right ordering of disputes over property. Personally, I always had in mind two major reforms for mountain Greece: a law prescribing eight hours' work for every man, instead of twelve for every woman, and prohibiting discussion of politics in the market-place during the hours of daylight; and, secondly, something like an inter-village football league to replace Venizelos and Pangalos and Metaxas as subjects for debate.[154] I know that this latter sounds a little jejune, like a joke from Beachcomber[155] or a

153 villages] typescript has 'villagers'.
154 Eleftherios Venizelos, Theodoros Pangalos, and Giannis Metaxas were all prominent and controversial figures in Greek politics in the years before and during WW2.
155 'Beachcomber' was the pen-name of English humorist J. B. Morton, who wrote regular comic columns for the *Daily Express* from the 1920s.

memorandum from the British Council, but I believe it to have possibilities.

But the Communism we knew in Greece never had any programme. The flippant suggestions of this foregoing paragraph would have been revolutionary, if only because they showed a practical interest in what might be done with Greece once the Germans had gone. The Communists of Greece possessed, on the other hand, a very remarkable technique for taking and holding power and a considerable ability in exploiting this technique.

I don't suppose Balkan politics have any great importance or interest to the outside world. Personalities and thumb-nail character sketches could occupy two pages of John Gunther[156] and leave the world more than satisfied. All that I am concerned with[157] writing about here is a form and technique of political organization that is probably not peculiar to Greece, that is generic to the world, and specific in its reflections on the way we live now.

The Communist party moved into the war when the Germans moved into Russia. In the dictator countries of Europe, like Greece, they had an organization that was already underground and habituated to working in the dark. Italians or Germans or state police made little difference to them. They could all be equally enemies or equally friends. They had heard too many

156 American journalist and author who wrote a popular book, *Inside Europe* (1936), drawing on his journalistic experiences while working for the *Chicago Daily News* in London, Paris, Berlin, Moscow, and Rome. He also spent some time in the Balkans.

157 with] typescript has 'with in'; 1st edn. has 'in'.

lies themselves to be overstrict in matters of propaganda. And, naturally, when the resistance started
they moved in and took charge of it.

The armies of Communism have a tougher and
stricter discipline than the Wehrmacht. In Lenin's day,
the party had room in it for discussion and argument.
If differences became too acute and on too serious a
matter, the party might split, but for the most part it
was evolutionary and tentative. It was feeling its way
and trying to look for facts, which, as Lenin remarked,
are stubborn things.[158] There is no longer any need
for nonsense of this kind. The Communists we knew
were organized to take and hold power and to get
orders and to carry them out. They would accept any
recruits that were prepared to accept their discipline
and any ideas or slogans that fitted the needs of the
moment.

We had been brought up, I suppose, in some kind
of liberal atmosphere, however incomplete. What
education we had tended to make us sceptical of
assertion and lovers of facts that could be proved. I
don't know whether the Germans first sanctioned a
completely amoral basis for propaganda, or whether
it goes back to Northcliffe,[159] or is really as old as the

---

158 'Facts are stubborn things' originally comes from John Adams's
    'Argument in Defence of the Soldiers in the Boston Massacre Trial',
    Dec. 1770. Lenin quotes it in an essay on Statistics and Sociology
    (Jan. 1917).
159 Lord Northcliffe (Alfred Harmsworth) was, like his brother Harold,
    an influential figure through his control of such newspapers as the
    London Evening News, the *Daily Mail* and *Daily Mirror*, and
    the *Times*. He was made a Viscount in 1917, and the following

history of men. In our time, and in the armies that have been fighting on our side, men have had still to be a little careful of their facts. Deliberate distortion has been dangerous. Even over-optimism and painting of the lily has been liable to censure. There has been a nice salt feeling among the united nations[160] that we would take our facts even if they were unpleasant.

No similar happy scruple, no inhibitions from an outdated form of education, hampered our comrades in the hills. They were clever men, speakers of many languages, well-travelled, and they looked on men and their emotions as something pliable to be moulded. They were experts in mass-meetings, coiners of slogans, which sometimes contradicted each other but were always temporarily effective. Early attempts at argument, misquotings, denials of something which we ourselves might have seen and have known to be true, soon persuaded us that we were working outside our charter and probably beyond our depth. We bought them into complaisance and left them free to run politics in the mountains so long as we were permitted—and it required permission—to fight Germans[161] on the railway line.

Personally, I got on well with the comrades, but then have[162] always felt it a weakness in myself to like and be attracted by too many different kinds of men. There were not many of them and they had an amusing

year accepted a post as Director of Propaganda in Lloyd George's Government.
160 united nations] 1st edn. capitalizes as 'United Nations'.
161 Germans] 1st edn. has 'the Germans'.
162 have] 1st edn. has 'I have'.

kind of cynicism. You always reckoned that there was a level somewhere on which you could do business. It was a compliment when one was finally accepted on this level and no longer assaulted by arguments of right or wrong or the needs of the Greek people, but could start at once on a practical basis and exchange of commodities.

Since they were few in number, they needed more than slogans to stay in power. Part of the technique was, therefore, what might be called mandatory, and the rest was physical. Ordinary society, and least of all a revolutionary army, have nothing that corresponds to a secret police and no way of fighting it. Two men in every village who are prepared to kill can hold the village. One political adviser beside every officer keeps the army in order. If the men that belong to this small internal organization, this army within the army, are ruthless enough, and if their discipline is good enough, they can always win.

Wives came to us from time to time and appealed to us to find their husbands, who had been taken at night and not heard of again. We had a friend in one village who helped us and was found one morning strangled with a piece of barbed wire. I guess he belonged to the wrong political party or got critical. It was not healthy to get out of line in mountain Greece.

We were fighting Germans, or trying to, or at least keeping that in front of us as a reason for being there. If the party compromised enough to let us do this —they made it fairly clear that it wasn't their primary object since the Germans, they reckoned, would go anyway, while others like the English or Americans might stay—I could find no quarrel with them. Personal preference might keep us away when they were beating a traitor (or more simply a political opponent), but Greek methods of torture are never very pleasant to watch, quite apart from any principle involved.

To those who came, often secretly, and complained of terrorism, we had only one answer. I believe it still to be a valid answer, though I am no longer so light-hearted about it. We said that the solution lay within their own hands, that no armed soldiers, no Allied divisions policing the country could correct this, only in the moral strength of individual men was there a solution. We told them that the men and officers of their own resistance movement were themselves terrorized and afraid to speak, and that while they stayed like this power would remain with those men who were strong enough to hold it.

This was an easy answer to give. You are Greeks, we told them, and we are English. We are here to fight Germans and have no politics. (Was this true or a lie? It was true when said personally, but in its wider applications[163] may have been falsified by events.) The politics of your own country, we said, are yours to make or mend. It was an easy answer, but cold comfort to a weeping woman. Once, I remember, in our small group, we got angry and stepped outside our charter. Something had stirred us, I forget which death or which barbarity, and we spoke frankly to a visiting

163 applications] 1st edn. has 'implications'.

delegate of the party. We told them that their slogans on anti-Fascism and freedom and democracy were a mockery, that the mountains held a worse tyranny than anything the Germans had imposed, a Fascism of the Left. I forget how the argument went after that, except that it was ugly, and that we ran a risk of being unable to continue those small and harmless operations against the Germans, which we prized then as the only justification for our existence in Greece. In the end we stayed on a basis of compromise.

But the truth, I think, is still valid. As I write this now, no real solution has come to Greece, nor to any part of civilized Europe. We have broken the terror of the Wehrmacht but have still to face the terror which overshadows men's lives. Democracy is no harlot on the streets, but, equally, Fascism is no piece of cardboard. Men who are strong and unscrupulous have learned a new and formidable technique of government. Propaganda and newspapers are small things. The common sense of ordinary, decent men will break them down. I would back the shrewd sagacity of a Greek mountain peasant to smell out most falsehoods. But behind this lies the second element of hard, physical power which can break an individual because it is organized and has discipline and knows no moral limits and has only one objective, to take power and keep it. I never lived in Chicago, but have a wide vicarious acquaintance from films and paperbacks of mobster-rule and gang-law. There isn't any fundamental difference in its application. It works with the same technique as the rule of Fascism of the Left or of the Right. Mostly, it comes down to cases with two strong-arm men who call round and offer a beating-up or a contribution to the party chest. Gang-law is weaker because it is local. The Fascisms of the Left and of the Right have flourished because they had some element of nationalism behind them. If Huey Long[164] could have got partners held together by some sort of spurious American philosophy in New York and Chicago, he might have lived longer.

164 A radical populist Democrat politician from Louisiana, Long served as Governor, and later as Senator until he was shot dead in 1935.

Chapter Eleven[165]

When we left Greece in November 1944 the sun was still shining, but roads and railways lay derelict. What destruction the Greeks had not achieved the Germans had completed more thoroughly, with more explosives and better technique. In Athens people were happy—and hungry. They were friendly, with the hospitality that is native to all Greeks, and tears came into their eyes because they no longer had anything in their houses to offer to English soldiers. Their country was ruined. Only Poland, perhaps, had suffered greater privation. The French, who spoke feelingly of the spiritual horrors of occupation, were children beside them. We left behind us, in the Sperkheios valley, fifty thousand homeless men and women and children. It was a mild autumn and the snows were late, which was a good thing, but the snows would have had to be late indeed to tide them over the period of civil war that followed.

When I came back to Greece, alone and not very willingly, in January of the New Year, the last year of the war, Athens was dark and silent. A cold curfew

165 Eleven] misnumbered as 'XII' in autograph addition to typescript.

closed down on the city with sunset. Stray shots broke the quiet of the long, dark, winter hours. In the streets were sad-faced men and women, still hungry and no longer happy. English soldiers moved with guns ready, as if in a hostile[166] land. Broken windows and shattered buildings and refuse in the streets, queues waiting for the bread ration, American journalists drinking noisily in the Grande Bretagne—you might ask yourself, being still of an inquiring nature, if this was the free Greece which we had toasted in rare, comfortable hours a year before. I don't know what we had expected then or what kind of mask we had thought the revolution might wear, but certainly not this antithesis of our dreams.

I found myself then with the melancholy task of trying to find and compensate those people who had been killed or crippled fighting for us during the occupation. There were a great many of them. It was beyond our powers to find and compensate the Greek nation. Some vast international organization might bring bread and build houses again for the wrecked peoples of the Sperkheios valley. For ourselves we had a simpler charter, to help those who had directly belonged to us and had fought and worked with us, and they alone were a large part of the best part of Greece. Some of those who had survived the Gestapo and the Security Police had killed each other[167] in the civil war. One of the best of these, who had dodged and

166 hostile] typescript has 'foreign'.
167 had killed each other] typescript originally read 'had been killed by the communists'. The revision is in Mulgan's hand.

fought the Germans from underground for two years was taken prisoner by the Communists and killed on a lonely piece of road by the village of Kiffisokhori, above Levadhia. The post-mortem report, when they brought his body back, described him as having been shot through the eye at fifteen feet, but I suppose in fact he was struck down by a power that is wider and more savage and more long-lasting. As the lights came on again in Athens, in well-to-do apartments, we heard many stories of Communist savagery. It wasn't so easy to extend sympathy to those who had lived comfortably under the Germans and were prepared to live the same way under any regime that would let them alone; but I could give all the sympathy that is in my heart for this man and many like him who had lived as patriots and been killed in the end by their own countrymen.

You could leave Greece with a certain impatience, saying to hell with a people that mutinied and caused revolutions at inopportune moments. We all felt like that often enough and each time were checked by some odd instance of individual greatness that could balance everything else.

An old man came in one day to our office.[168] He was lame and one eye was half-closed with a discoloration that looked permanent. He was half-shaven and about sixty years of age, and part-crippled as he was, nevertheless filled the office so that you could feel there was a man there among smaller men. We left the

168 Identified in *Long Journey to the Border* (p. 334) as Janni Fafoutis.

office and went out to have a drink together because
a military office is no place to entertain friends. I
wanted to hear his story, because that was the work
I was doing then,[169] not for any reason that I wanted
to hear picturesque adventures of the underground,
but because we needed all these facts for our records.
I asked him questions about this person and that and
about dates, until he grew impatient and pushed both
our glasses aside and leaned one hand on the table
resting his wounded eye and began to tell me this
story. He spoke in bad English the way I have tried
to write it down here, because it pleased him to be
able to speak in English and not to have to rely on my
broken understanding of his Greek.

'Listen, boy,' he said, 'it was Euboea, the winter,
the February of 1942. All of Euboea was covered
with snow. It was a cold winter, the first winter of the
occupation in Greece. Shepherd came to me one day,
said there are for three days in Kazarma, on the other
side of the wild rocky mountains, forty kilometres
from my village, there are there waiting eight men,
that might be English. So I took my eldest son and
shepherd and I and my son went and found these eight
men. Yes, they were Englishmen all right, they were
Australians and New Zealanders and they wanted to
get out, they wanted to get out of Greece and get to
Cairo. So I said all right, I said, "Come with me"
and we marched back those forty kilometres over the
same mountains until came[170] to the sea again. We

169 because that . . . doing then] omitted from 1st edn.
170 came] 1st edn. has 'we came'.

left the cave where they had been hiding and we left the shepherd's hut and we came back to my house by the sea. It was late at night when we came there and we were tired. But the next day the sea was very wild and so I kept these eight men, these Australians and New Zealanders, five days in my house. Each day we looked out and the sea was wild. But on the sixth day, the sea went down and I and the men, these same eight men, went down to the sea-shore. I put the men in my boat and we went to Skyros. That was an easy journey. It was an easier journey than walking over the mountains. There I gave them to a man in Skyros that was a friend of mine and he agreed that he would take them across the sea to Smyrna. So I left them there and a few days later I had a letter from them saying that they had got safely to Smyrna, yes they had got back safely to Smyrna and afterwards to Cairo so for that I was grateful.'

Once the old man started talking I had as much chance of stopping him as I had of arresting the war. He went on:

'So it was the March of the same year, 1942. There were Germans and Italians, but more Italians, all over Euboea, and one day a man came to my house and said we must prepare things for the coming of aeroplanes. They will send aeroplanes now, he said, that will drop arms and explosives with parachutes. So I said, all right, but why have you come to me? And he said they gave me your name in Cairo as a good man and a patriot and a trustworthy person, and I laughed at him then for I had never been to

Cairo, and asked him what kind of system is this
that they have in Cairo. But he said, that is all right,
they know all about you in Cairo. Well, he stayed
in my house three days. The fourth day at midnight
we were waiting on top of the hill above my house,
I tell you it was no child's play that winter, it was a
very cold winter, the first and coldest winter of the
war, when we heard the coming of aeroplanes. At
once we started signals, lighted fires, flashed torches,
the way this man from Cairo said. Nothing happened
but there was an explosion down by the village. First
aeroplane came over and second aeroplane and we
could not see anything drop, not one thing. So I go
down to the village and there are all my people very
frightened from the explosion. So I explained to them
what was happening and at once old men and young
men and children came out into the hills above the
village and found all the parachutes, yes every one.
We were working all night and by morning nothing
was left there showing and everything was gathered
in. But there was one tragedy and mistake, I will tell
you frankly,' he said, 'since you are here to find out
about mistakes and to look after people that suffered,
there were some parachutes that were dropped a long
way away and two poor shepherds that knew nothing
about all this were looking at them next morning
when the Italians found and shot them. Well, I
suppose that is war, yes, for the innocent and guilty
and unsuspecting.

   'So early next morning, while we were still
gathering up everything that we had found, my friend

that had come from Cairo said to me, was looking everywhere and last found it and called to me, Janni, here are the most important things, and opened a barrel and pulled out four magnetic charges like turtles. These are what I want, he said, and must be brought to my house in Athens. Well, I gave him my promise then but it was not an easy thing and I was thinking to myself where all this would end that had started with the eight Englishmen that I sent out to Cairo because I was loving them and all Englishmen and wanting to help them. So two days later, I called two[171] young men from my village and we set out together. Each one of us carried one of these turtles in a small bag and in turn each one of us carried the fourth. We went over the mountains by paths that only I know. We crossed the sea with a small rowing-boat and arrived to the coast of Attica and from there through forests and rocky hills, always night, and going alone, and arrived in Athens. We went straight to his house, to this Cairo friend of mine. You understand that this was the first time that I had met him but passing those nights together waiting for the aeroplane I got to know him well and realize that he was a good friend. So this was a big success, us getting there with the four turtles. After that you will have read all about it, how they sank two large steamers with them in the Piraeus. I do not remember the names any longer of the steamers because after my illness, I have lost a little bit of the

---

171 two] typescript has 'three'. This must be a mistake, since there are clearly only three people in total carrying the four turtles.

memory that I had, but other people will remember them.

'Well, that was not my work, the sinking of the ships, but other men. Some of them were afterwards killed, good men. I started back the same night, by the same paths, the way we had come to Athens, 215 kilometres, but we shortened it a little bit from the paths that only I was knowing, and finally we got back to our village at midnight, the fourth night. Well, we needed some rest then but two days later had a note from a friend, you will know his name so I do not need to tell it to you, saying come to Athens quick, so left again footing all the way. Travel from Euboea to Athens was forbidden by the Italians then. May they rest happily all the Italians that died in Greece, they caused us much trouble. But at night-time, travelling, there was no difficulty for they stayed in their barracks all the night. So three days later I was at my friend's house in Athens, early in the morning. He was sleeping when I got there but he came out quick. He told me that there were thirteen Englishmen that I must take to a boat waiting for them on the east coast on the south of Euboea. We took breakfast together and I said, "There is not time to waste, we must start quick." So eight o'clock that night, darkness, we left Athens and came to Porto Rafti. Quick, quick we went in a small boat from there. It was dark yet, still one hour and a half when we reached Euboea. We had no time to lose. We landed and travelled through bushy hills and little rivers and reached the place where the *caïque* was waiting. The boat was there and the captain said, start at once. In fifteen minutes they left for the coast of Turkey. I myself said good-bye to them and spent all the day in a friend's house near there and the next day after eleven hours' walking came back to my home.

'Quiet then for some time. June 1942, summer-time, shepherd—same shepherd—brought by secret ways five New Zealanders to my house. So I called my friend, the captain, and he said O.K. and they set off and arrived safely.

'July 1942 came two men to[172] my house. They knew all about me. I was not surprised any longer, yes, I said laughing, I have many friends in Cairo. They wanted to go to Athens so I took them the same long way and we got to Athens without accident. They said nothing to me of their work, and that was all right, it was not my work, and when we got to Patissia, said they, all right, now we know where we are, good night and thank you, friend, we shall see you another time, but I have never seen them again.

'August and September and October, many Englishmen and New Zealanders and Australians. I cannot remember their names but they are written down somewhere. And then November and the priest, my friend, from the village two kilometres away, sent me a note, saying come at once. So I went and there was with him a man unknown to me. The priest took me up to him. "There are no names here," he said, "but this is my friend." We shook hands. "This is my friend," the priest said, "that has come from Cairo."

172 to] typescript has 'from'.

So I asked him, what can I do for you, and he told me, you can do much. There will come a submarine, he said, in a few days near here with many things that are needed, rifles and ammunition and explosives. So I left him there and went back to my village. My village is a very small village, there are not many people in it, no more than forty, men, women, and children. I called the young men together and told them of this thing and straight away they said, "with you to the death, father". So we went then together, down to the shore where the submarine would come. The weather was very bad, rainy and stormy. The winter was setting in. We sheltered in a cave by the shore. The friend from Cairo joined us and we lit fires for the submarine, all the night we kept the fire[173] burning but no submarine came. Night came again and we made the same signals but nothing came and so we went home. The young men were sad and cold and hungry, for like all young men they were impatient. Three days later, came a messenger to me with a note from my friend the bishop. The submarine had come but to the wrong beach ten miles to the north and with it had landed three men and had unloaded all the stores from the submarine into a cave by the shore. Straight away I knew where this was, for I am an old man and have lived a long time there and know the coast well. So I called my young men again together and we set off. The weather was very bad, rain and storm to beat the hell. And after five hours we came to this cave and lit a fire there. We were very hungry so broke open the

173 fire] 1st edn. has 'fires'.

stores and found biscuits. Next morning, sent two of the young men back home and they brought a boat and rowed it round to the bay where the cave was. Weather was still stormy. We loaded the boat and set out, left two men behind to rest and guard the stores that we could not take. We rowed for two miles and the sea got more wild. Our boat went up to the sky and the water came in, the boat was half-filled with sea. In the end we reached there, the small bay by my home and pulled the boat up on the beach and unloaded the stores. We were all trembling with cold and carried up the stores into the cave. Here I got a rupture, first it was as big as an almond but now is as big as an egg.'

All the time that he was talking and telling me this he never stopped. I have tried to set it down as he told it to me, not for any particular reason except that he had some virtue that was Homeric and simple that I can only recapture by reporting him faithfully. He went on:

'Three of the boys went up to the village and brought us dry clothes and also two chickens, cooked, and potatoes and wine. While we were sitting round the fire getting dry, the boys said with one voice, "Let us go and bring here the rest of the stores and our comrades so that we can eat together." The weather was good by then and the sea went down so they left and by half-past three they were back again, all glad, and in ten minutes' time all the stores were in the cave and all start singing. In the meantime, I had cooked dinner, yes we were happy then, the boys singing and dancing till morning. The day seemed to be calm, and suddenly with one voice the boys said: "Where is this hero, your friend, that came from Cairo?" So we all laughed then, yes, he was not down with us wading in the sea but sleeping safely with my other friend the priest.

'Well, a week later, sent a messenger and took all the stores from the cave and sent them by boat to Piraeus and no thanks and never saw them again.'

He pulled our two glasses back into the centre of the table.

'I don't remember well any longer', he said, 'after the Germans caught me and beat me, my eye hurts me, and I do not remember. But I remember that I went thirteen times the road from my village to Athens and brought out many men.'

I suppose you can get irritated with the Greek people and despair of them and even get killed by them, but never entirely forsake them while there exist men like this one-eyed pirate who are prepared to fight on our side.

Chapter Twelve[174]

We spent a lot of time during the war talking about the world after the war. Some of this discussion was organized by the Army on highly creditable lines but, as usually happens, the basic conclusions were arrived at more crudely and personally. There seemed to be a good deal of agreement. If I summarize the conclusions here with an equal crudity, it isn't done in entire forgetfulness of the complex issues that are involved in some of the simple things that simple people ask for. Unfortunately, when demands are simple and easily understood, it is more difficult to refuse them or to explain that they are impractical. There was a certain amount of good sense in these conversations all the same. I don't know how much will be granted to the men I heard talking but I know that they will require some persuasion before they abandon what they ask for, and it is just as well to bear these things in mind when alternative programmes are being offered or civil discipline is being called in to enforce the dissuasion.

174 Chapter Twelve] no heading or number in typescript.

It is probably not true that everyone ought to be happy. Happy is one of the foolish words that are destroyed by usage. Love is not a word of that kind since it is a name for something that really occurs and every hundredth man realizes this and hands the word on full of meaning. But if everyone cannot be happy, they can feel well in themselves at some time in their lives, not merely physically well, but quite casually, as it might be sleepy with sunshine or drinking with friendly people. In equating sadness and loneliness and strife, it is proper to remember that the conditions of living are fulfilled when everyone has the opportunity (as they have not had the opportunity) at some time in their lives to feel well and happy in themselves.

Most of the men that I knew asked for very little beyond this. Every sensible man wants a home and the woman that he wants to live with and room for his children to move in. And besides that he wants some work to do. It does not matter at all what the work is, whether it is making roads or making books, although it is better if it is work that he can do satisfactorily and with belief. There will be great pleasure for him if the work is of a kind that he knows to be required by the people he meets, and if occasionally they will say to him, 'That's good road-making', or 'The books are better this year.' I never found any work, down to cleaning pigsties in which I was once heavily engaged, where there wasn't some degree of specialization and aptitude which could mark a man out, not necessarily for more pay but for reputation and respect among his fellows. And an old Greek who guided us once in heavy mist over Agrafa, and who was, I should guess, pre-eminent in that region for moroseness and stupidity, broke a silence of several hours to say, 'There's no one else in my village could have found the way on a day like this', and spat twice and went on walking while we slogged after him respectfully.

If there are people who are ordering and arranging this work, as in nearly all kinds of work there will be, that also is quite all right with most of us so long as there is point and reason in the orders. If for[175] any reason some unpleasant fellow starts giving the orders, he should be told quietly to go. The English are very good at getting rid of unpleasant foremen and overseers by some kind of silent pressure. They stand up better than most to the small tyranny of small men. What happens to small and unpleasant men when they are dispensed with doesn't matter, unless they all get together in one country, or form a new political party in our own—and I think we can deal with that situation too if the need arises.

Most men are not averse to a good deal of organization in their work. The work itself, in most cases, will not be satisfactory unless it is organized and given point. Where nobody wants the organization is in his own home. This was the beautiful and basic truth with which most of the discussions I assisted at

175 for] typescript originally had 'by', revised to 'for'; 1st edn. has 'by'.

began and ended. This is what most ordinary men have in their minds when they talk about liberty.

Liberty has a French rather than an English sound. The English are more interested in the practice than the conception. Freedom of speech is a good thing for those that want to make speeches, but we shall not have time for much of that—a certain amount of discussion in the public-house perhaps, but that counts as home. But most of us will have work to do and little time for theories, and will be ready to let those who are skilled at making speeches and organizing and giving the orders, go ahead. So long as they are efficient and competent, that will be all right. If they are not efficient nor competent, then I imagine this sad truth could be pointed out to them by some means like an election or an occasional deputation. Men are not any longer prepared for the inefficient and incompetent to flourish by birthright or because they have friends in committee. A certain amount of this abides in all systems, but I formed the impression that the barrack-room speakers from England will be less tolerant of it now than they have been in the past.

In a future English world, I can see men arguing, men skilled in debate, and correspondence columns filled with controversy on the development of an educational system, the better organization of public utilities, implementing of legislation, trades union congresses and civic rights. I can foresee all that, easily enough. I can see it all being done for the most part by other people than those with whom I discussed these things, by people who are good at this sort of work and who care about it. The rest of us will, on the whole, be tolerant of mistakes, if they are made in good faith and by people who are working earnestly. It is not true that the road to hell is paved with good intentions. We have been some way down the road to hell as a community and we have seen who did the paving. The groundwork of this royal road was laid by the ignorant and oblivious; the tarmac trimmings and sidewalks were added by smart fellows who cashed in on a deteriorating contract.

There is, nevertheless, little to be gained from trying to make us into good citizens who will be qualified and interested enough to express an opinion on every issue. We are informed enough to lay down the general directive but beyond that we should never be very successful. Politics are better left to the earnest professionals. What we can offer is a desire to work very hard and a willingness to fight at any time for a home with people that we like, and freedom within it.

They say that in the Spanish Civil War the Basques fought best when their women were near enough to bring up the midday meal. This may be very true, but there are unfortunately few wars where a man can take his wife with him. It has been the great strength of England's civilian war that men and women who cared for each other have been able to fight it side by side. For the rest of us, these years will be remembered as the time of the great separation when there were no more families and no more homes, when men and women worked for the most part a long way away from each other and only occasionally met to kiss good-bye.

Living away from people that you like is not very satisfactory. It is not the best way to live nor the one that many people would choose. It gives men a measure, nevertheless, of the things that they want in the world. In the days when everybody that could afford it had a home and lived with the person that they cared about, it was possible to take a good deal of this for granted. And if you looked round the public-house on Saturday night and saw the couples sitting contentedly, you would say these people were perhaps wasting their time, being neither very exciting nor obviously creative. There was no need to take account then of the strength of affection that was between these people or the total amount of casual happiness that there might be in their lives. But now, looking back, you would say that in all the evils that existed then, the fondness that people had for one another was always good.

You don't need to be very clever to love someone. It is better not to be clever. The people who are simple and honest have a great advantage here. Anyone who imagines that rough and conventionally educated[176] people don't understand these things, should live with them for a while, or censor soldiers' letters. These latter often know very much more about these things than do the sophisticated and the intelligent and the self-conscious.

---

176 conventionally educated] 1st edn. has 'comparatively uneducated'.

There is a lot of luck in being able to live with someone that you care about. It is not a very easy thing to do, for example, on 33s. 6d. a week in a back street of Durham. When you consider all the obstacles that a kindly society tended to put in one's way, it is remarkable that so many people achieved it. And when you have considered this, and studied the reality of this affection that is in people around you, now that war has taught us this lesson, then you are apt to think that the most important conclusion for this war is the creation of a country where these people will be able to live happily together again.

This is perhaps why nobody is greatly stirred when they see the blue-prints of the new era with their wide concrete drives and central heating and communal laundry. These things will be very nice when they arrive, but any home will be all right in the meantime where there is liberty and enough security to be with the people that you care about. And the young man and the girl from the back street of Durham are not greatly concerned with the architectural splendours of the new world. You could buy them off a lot more cheaply than that if you wanted to. All that they are requiring now is any home that is not entirely dirt and squalor, and enough food so that they do not always have to be remembering that they are hungry, and enough time to realize that they are happy at last, and enough security to know that there will be work next week as well as this. When they have been given this much—and it doesn't sound a great deal, considered carefully—it will be possible to interest them in some more generalized project. But for the duration of this long war, the man and girl in the back streets of Durham, and the soldier who goes to bed in barracks, and his girl who works at munitions a long way away, are not making heavy imaginative demands on the future rulers of their country.

The basic liberty that people refer to when they use the term, which is not often, is the liberty to live in peace with the person that they care for in an ordinary and very satisfying way. There are other components of liberty but this is the most important one, and the difficulty that arises is that those who are chosen to make the speeches are not always talking and thinking in terms of the necessary simplicity, so that when they talk about liberty or democracy there is no certainty in the minds of these others that they are referring to what is important to them. But if it is made clear that liberty and democracy mean enough security and peace to share our lives with the people that we care about, then there will be no doubt that it is liberty and democracy that we want. If we can have the freedom to love someone that is sufficient to begin with.

On the other hand there are certain manifestations of individual liberty with which we can easily dispense. The liberty of the Birmingham small arms manufacturers to sell Hitler fifty million pounds'[177] worth of arms in 1934, for example.[178] This kind of

177 fifty million pounds] 1st edn. has 'millions of pounds'.
178 example] Mulgan had originally added 'just enough to take the Reichswehr into the Rhineland and no more'. The line is struck

liberty that exercises itself on the platform of John Stuart Mill is a luxury that can be set aside without undue hardship. There was a young Frenchman in Paris, the Christmas of 1938, who spoke at some length on this subject. Being a stranger to us, he told us these things, dark-eyed and eloquent, in the way that you might tell a stranger something that touched you closely. For when he was mobilized, he said, in the hollow crisis of that autumn, he went to Forsbach in front of the Maginot Line, and lay there in a gun-pit, shivering through the autumn nights, waiting the order to fire. And night after night, the steel trains thundered across the frontier, fulfilling the last orders of Schneider-Creuzot for Thyssen or Krupps.[179] Nearly all other traffic was suspended but the steel trains went through unimpeded, answering the orders of a greater power than any he was called upon to die for. So he had come back after that mobilization, not quite so enamoured of *la patrie,* and it was clear as he leant across the table, telling us this with many a vigorous gesture, that when the next mobilization came, he would not go back to Forsbach with quite the same *élan* and nobility and desperation for the sacred causes[180] of *la belle France.* It seemed possible from what he said that he would not go back to Forsbach at all.

---

through in the typescript.

179 Schneider-Creuzot was a French manufacturer of armaments, accused by Paul Faure (a member of the Chambre des Députés), of financing Hitler. Thyssen and Krupps were leading industrial families in Germany.

180 causes] 1st edn. has 'cause'.

This, in fact, is the kind of liberty that we can do very well without. When Mr. Hoover, who once did so much to relieve the Belgians and suppress the Russians, says that 'the fourth freedom', economic freedom,[181] needs resuscitating, he is not talking to us. It is not clear exactly to whom he is talking, but it is certainly not to us.

No one of us, talking sensibly, discounts the frustrations of this future that we plan. Few of us expect it to be materially different in outward form or in human anxiety. But the simple desires which have been outlined above, we are prepared to work for, and to fight for, to fight anyone for; so that our children should know struggle but not war, and trouble but not passion.

In the English mind, there is a breeding ground for quiet, contented beliefs. One of them is that we always win the wars. Another, that war ends and life begins again in a similar pattern, the same house, the same wife, the same foreman.[182] But into this last belief there have crept strange elements of doubt. For the house has in some cases been bombed, and the foreman grown old or dead or gone away, and the wife is still there but she is a long way away and the children are growing up unfamiliarly. So that there steal over this native pattern of the recurring past new

181 Mulgan is presumably thinking of a speech Herbert Hoover made on 16 Sept. 1941. Warning against entry to the war, Hoover added to Roosevelt's 'Four Freedoms' 'a fifth freedom. That is economic freedom', which for Hoover explicitly included freedom 'to accumulate property [and] freedom of private enterprise'.
182 foreman] the typescript has 'foremen'.

shades and colours, interesting but disquieting. And in consequence we hold very firmly to the lines of the pattern that are still recognizable and that represent stubbornly formed desires, that belong very definitely to the past and will endure into the future.

These are the counsels of sobriety but at all times the lines of the pattern persist.

Few Englishmen are revolutionary in their instincts. We may sometimes, in bitter days, have wished that they were more so, but in the long range of history their attitude to political matters has had great value. (Even the arrogant boys from the colonies and the great Americas[183] will admit this if you give them enough to drink.) In general, it seems that the bloodthirsty figure which was conjured up for election time was more or less imaginary. It was part of a general ignorance as to how most of the country lived and thought. Part of it was a wistful desire for more flagrant opposition than the Trades Unions provided, like the old women in *Don Juan* who walked in the captured town asking when the raping was going to begin.[184]

The English have nevertheless learned to be more dogmatic and sombre in their demands. They would resent any anarchic period of transition, prefer by instinct the gradualness for which they are historically famous. But if there were no alternative,

183 Americas] 1st edn. has 'Americans'.
184 See Canto VIII, stanza CXXXII, in which certain 'buxom, middle-aged' women (rather than Mulgan's old women) were heard to wonder 'wherefore the ravishing did not begin.'

no way of breaking down the oblivion of those who govern them, I feel that they might now choose more desperate courses. The afflictions of England were matters not only of economics but also of understanding. The most deadly part of human life, the sorrow that Karl Marx felt like a scourge, was this oblivion that clouds the understanding of the well-possessed. If the English can effect among themselves a general tolerance and understanding, they will continue to deserve the rare praise of an ironic world.

It is a sad commentary on human values that war which has accustomed us to death should have brought with it so full and rich a sense of life. Death and decay came on the Germans when they lost this sense of living. When they knew that they were leaving Greece they took men from the Aevroff prison and shot them in a series of stubborn massacres that lasted for several days. I have no doubt that they left the same bitter trail all over Europe. I had the melancholy duty after they had gone of visiting and talking to the families of some of these men that they killed. The men who were killed had been *saboteurs,* or gleaners of information for the Allies, patriots in their own quiet and dangerous way. They had been soldiers in a kind of war that is outlawed by the Hague Convention but is in fact as real and as deadly as any open warfare. It was hard to understand the mentality of these Germans who had taken the time to kill some hundreds of men long after the necessity for reprisals had passed. There is something to be said for the technique of reprisal when a country is being occupied. It is a cruel technique but effective. But when you are leaving a country, there is no longer any need to kill men, merely for the sake of killing. When the Germans were on their outward wave of conquest, there was an argument for nearly everything they did, down to the graveyards of Poznán. But on the way home, the long trek back, with everything lost and German destiny revealed for a dark perspective of defeat, there was no longer any need for this killing, only the desire that must have been in their hearts to bring down as much human life as they could in their own ruin and retreat.

For ourselves, we have been the gainers from this war. We have seen a good deal of death but have learnt by contrast to appreciate the living. Each spring now has promise for us. Not all of us were family men by instinct, but are friendly now and made happy by every small child that we see, for the new generations that are coming on to support us. The sparse green of Attica and rare fruit blossoms[185] in the city of Athens never looked or smelled sweeter in all their long history than they did in the last spring of the great European War when we began to make plans for a new Europe and a new world.

The years that are coming now are as full of promise as of difficulty. They hold in prospect as much demand on humanity as did the years of war. There are no simple solutions but there are at least simple beliefs. We have agreement at heart, if not entirely

185 rare fruit blossoms] 1st edn. has 'the rare fruit blossoms'.

in method. As one who found war interesting, if not entirely acceptable, I would like to end by subscribing to the view that we are not likely to find time lying heavy on our hands in an immediate future of armed peace and tentative experiment.

Index of Names and Places